BLUEPRINT
FOR INCLUSION

A Practical Guide to Supporting Students with IEPs in the General Education Classroom

REBEKAH POE, M. ED.

Blueprint for Inclusion

Published by TeacherGoals Publishing, LLC Beech Grove, IN
www.teachergoals.com
Cover Design by: Tricia Fuglestad and Caroline Gray
Interior Design by: Zoe Howard
Edited by: Carrie Turner and Katie Gray

Library of Congress Control Number: 9781959419280
Paperback ISBN: 978-1-959419-28-0
ASIN: B0F3Y2KC2T

First Printing April 2025

PRAISE FOR *BLUEPRINT FOR INCLUSION*

Rebekah has done something extraordinary with this book. She has crafted a masterpiece that seamlessly combines an authentic practitioner's perspective with evidence-based research that speaks to all stakeholders in the education space. Woven throughout are policies and effective practices that can help teachers of all experiences, parents, and administrators navigate the complex and often misunderstood world of IEPs. This is the type of book that should be top of the list for book studies and educator training.

Dr. Adam Dovico
Professor, Former Principal, Author, and Speaker

As a multi-decade educator and a parent of a neurodivergent child, I wholeheartedly recommend Rebekah Poe's book, *Blueprint for Inclusion: A Practical Guide to Supporting Students with IEPs in the General Education Classroom*! It needs to be in every school, teaching credential program, and family library for those who have children with IEPs. Inclusion and special education programs are complicated and overwhelming, but Poe brings clarity and solutions for the educator and parent alike.

Dean Deaver
Elementary School Principal, Father of a Neurodivergent Child

This book is very well-written and will be beneficial to teachers, especially those who are joining our profession with little to no explicit training in educational pedagogy, as they navigate the work of reaching our students who learn in different ways and/ or who would benefit from the different supports included in their IEPs. The author combines precise legal information with practical classroom strategies in a way that is both thought-provoking and heartfelt with a touch of humor sprinkled throughout. The examples of how she collaborated with others as well as the resource examples that are included will serve to enhance teachers' ability to use this book and, ultimately, help all students have the inclusive classroom environments they ALL deserve.

Dr. Tara M. Foster, Ph.D, NBCT
Educational Consultant with Experience as a Regional Coordinator,
Classroom Teacher & School Administrator

Blueprint for Inclusion is a leading-edge and heartfelt guide for all parties aspiring to support students in an authentically inclusive classroom environment. Through an additive and collaborative mindset, Rebekah Poe skillfully navigates us through successful strategies backed by research while mindfully unpacking the nuances for student success.

Derrick Carlson, M.Ed.
Classroom Teacher

Blueprint for Inclusion is an essential read for educators at every stage of one's career— preservice, new, or veteran. Poe demystifies the complexities of IDEA and special education with clarity and practicality. By seamlessly blending legal insights, research, and real-world understanding, this book provides a comprehensive yet accessible guide that empowers educators to navigate special education effectively. This is a must-have resource for anyone committed to fostering inclusion and equity in education.

Meghan Allen, M.Ed, NBCT
Special Education Teacher, Alabama's Elementary Teacher of the Year 2018

In *Blueprint for Inclusion*, Rebekah Poe offers an invaluable resource for educators seeking to create more inclusive learning environments for students with Individualized Education Programs (IEPs). Drawing from her extensive experience as an educator and advocate for special education, Poe combines practical strategies with compassionate insights, making this guide an essential addition to any teacher's professional library.

This guide doesn't shy away from addressing challenges, but Poe's encouraging tone inspires confidence. Educators will walk away not only with strategies but with a renewed sense of purpose in their mission to support diverse learners.

For anyone committed to building more inclusive classrooms, *Blueprint for Inclusion* is a must-read. It's practical, heartfelt, and profoundly relevant in today's educational landscape.

Leslie Hinton, Ed. S.
Assistant Principal and Former Special Education Lead
Teacher and Department Chair

Blueprint for Inclusion is an inspiring and practical guide that demonstrates how to create inclusive classrooms where all students, regardless of ability, thrive. With real-life examples, proven strategies, and a focus on collaboration, the author highlights the many benefits of inclusion for both students with disabilities and their peers. The book emphasizes that accommodations do not diminish academic rigor and offers simple, actionable strategies to motivate disengaged students. A must-read for both new and experienced educators, this book provides essential insights and tools for fostering an inclusive environment where every student can succeed.

Dr. Gayle Gober, Ed. D.
Education Consultant and Retired Secondary School Administrator

Blueprint for Inclusion is an invaluable resource for educational leaders and teachers to meet the needs of all students. It provides comprehensive strategies, tools, and frameworks to foster inclusive learning environments. The book combines ideas with actionable steps, including collaboration between general and special education staff. Real-life examples illustrate how to implement effective teaching practices that promote equity and inclusivity. A must-read for educators dedicated to supporting all learners.

Dr. Tron Young
Administrator

Blueprint for Inclusion is a great guide for general education teachers to better understand special education as a whole and tangible ways to collaborate with all stakeholders for the success of their students receiving special education services. Poe highlights the importance of inclusion through specific ideas classroom teachers can implement to better support their students with diverse needs and personal anecdotes. In a sentiment: all students are OUR students and it's our responsibility to ensure they are receiving the support they need to be successful.

Dr. Shane Saeed
Elementary ELA Curriculum Coordinator, author, and national presenter

To my students— past, present, and future. You are my why.

To Dr. Gayle Gober and Marrianne Hayward. Thank you for seeing something in me and pushing me to be more. I wouldn't be here without you.

To my friends. Thank you for your unwavering support.

To my family. Thank you for your unconditional love, patience, understanding, and encouragement.

TABLE OF CONTENTS

Introduction 11
Acronyms and Terms to Know 13
Chapter 1: Let's Talk IDEA 17
History of IDEA 17
Pillars of IDEA 19
    Pillar 1: Free Appropriate Public Education (FAPE) 19
    Pillar 2: Appropriate Evaluation 20
    Pillar 3: Individualized Education Plan/Program (IEP) 20
    Pillar 4: Least Restrictive Environment or LRE 22
    Pillar 5: Parent Participation 23
    Pillar 6: Procedural Safeguards 24
Chapter 2: Special Education Eligibility 25
The Referral Process 25
Evaluation for Eligibility 29
    Specific Learning Disability 29
    Other Health Impairment 29
    Speech and Language Impairment 30
    Autism 30
    Emotional Disturbance 31
    Visual Impairment, Including Blindness 32
    Hearing Impairment and Deafness 32
    Deaf-Blindness 33
    Orthopedic Impairment 33
    Intellectual Disability 33
    Traumatic Brain Injury 35
    Multiple Disabilities 36
Understanding Students with IEPs 36
    High Incidence Disabilities 36
    Medium Incidence Disabilities 37
    Low Incidence Disabilities 38
Chapter 3: Defining Inclusive Education and its Benefits 38
Benefits to Students in Special Education 38
    Peer Role Models 38
    Language and Communication 41
    Social Skills 43
    Increased Achievement of IEP Goals 44
    Standards-Aligned Instruction 44
    Increased Staff Collaboration 45

Benefits to Students in General Education.................................... 46
Increased Understanding and Acceptance of Diversity 46
Greater Academic Outcomes 48
Opportunities to Master Activities by Practicing and Teaching Others 48
All Students' Needs Are Better Met 49

Chapter 4: Motivating Reluctant Learners 51
Chapter 5: Creating an Inclusive Classroom Environment 55
Collaboration.. 55
Authenticity.. 57
Relevance 60
Engagement 65

Chapter 6: Collaborative Teamwork...................................... 69
Building Effective Partnerships with Teachers and Families 70
Communicating with Other Teachers.................................... 70
Communicating with Families... 71
Positive Communication for Positive Relationships 72
Troubleshooting Communication Problems 74
Co-Teaching: Roles and Design 74
Co-Teaching Models.. 75
Co-Teaching Strategies.. 80

Chapter 7: Differentiating Instruction 83
Differentiating Instruction... 83
Differentiation in the Environment 84
Differentiation in the Content 87
Differentiation in the Instructional Process............................ 90
Differentiation in the Product 92
Differentiation and Universal Design for Learning 95

Chapter 8: Accommodations & Modifications 99
Instruction..101
Assessment 101
Accessibility..101
Behavioral/Sensory 102
Common Accommodations..103
Selecting and Implementing Appropriate Accommodations 104
Selecting Accommodations 105
Implementing Accommodations 107
Evaluating Accommodations 109
Making Modifications..110
Differentiation Versus Accommodations Versus Modifications ...110

When Are Modifications Appropriate? 111
Chapter 9: Multisensory Instructional Approaches 113
What is Multisensory Learning? 113
Multisensory Learning vs Learning Styles...................................113
Benefits of Multisensory Learning for Students with Disabilities.........115
Strategies for Incorporating Multisensory Approaches into Lessons .. 117
Ideas for Multisensory Instruction in Phonological Awareness...... 117
Ideas for Multisensory Instruction in Math................................ 119
Other Ideas for Multisensory Instruction—No physical
materials necessary! 121
Chapter 10: Assessing Progress and Monitoring IEP Goals............123
What method will you use for progress monitoring?.....................123
How often are you going to conduct progress monitoring? 125
How will you collect progress monitoring data? 127
Using Progress Monitoring Data to Inform Decisions....................129
1. Identify Patterns and Trends 131
2. Adjust Instructional Strategies 131
3. Modify IEP Goals and Services 131
4. Collaborate with the IEP Team 132
Chapter 11: Navigating Challenges and Overcoming Barriers..........133
Establishing Expectations 133
Strategies for addressing behavior issues and promoting
self-regulation 136
Understanding Behavior as Communication 136
Factors that Contribute to Student Behavior...........................137
Determining the Function of Student Behavior 140
Behavior Strategies and Interventions by Function 142
Chapter 12: De-escalating Students in Crisis 147
D is for Describe What you See 149
I is for Inquire about a Feeling..150
V is for Verify the Details and Validate the Feeling 151
E is for Explore Solutions 152
Restore 152
Addressing the Aftermath..153
Punishments vs Consequences 153
Disproportionality in School Discipline...................................155
Restorative Practices...155
Conclusion...159

INTRODUCTION

DEAR READER,

In your hands you hold my heart and soul. At least that's how it feels. I have spent the entirety of my adult life working to support and teach students of every age and ability. It's been a season of growth—a time for learning, unlearning, and gaining clarity on what truly works and what doesn't. And that process is never ending. But in my teaching tenure, I have learned the true meaning and importance of inclusion is to ensure that each student is able to achieve their personal best. And reader, it is not something that can be done alone. It takes collaboration. It takes understanding. It takes a willingness to go against what has "always been done" in an effort to make the positive changes that will transform not only your classroom, but the lives of the students who fill it.

> " Every single student in your classroom has the right to be there. "

The first thing to remember is that every single student in your classroom has the right to be there. To be taught by you. All students, even students with IEPs, are general education students first. In 2022, UNICEF estimated that there are approximately 240 million children with disabilities globally. In the US alone, there are 7.3 million students enrolled in public schools who have disabilities, making up 15% of the national school enrollment during the 2021 school year (PewResearch, 2023). That percentage varies widely depending on what state you are in with the greatest percentage being in New York (20.5%) and the smallest percentage residing in Hawaii (11.3%).

Most students in the US with disabilities will receive most of their instruction in the general education classroom. Students with disabilities such as specific learning disabilities (SLD), speech and language impairments (SLI), and Other Health Impairments (OHI), spend much of their day learning alongside their typical peers in a general education classroom—your classroom. They might receive special education services from a special education teacher or

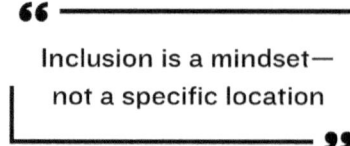

> Inclusion is a mindset—
> not a specific location

a Speech Language Pathologist (SLP) within your classroom, as well. It's a myth that students receiving special education must receive services in a separate setting. And as such, a majority of the students' time will be spent with you and within your general education classroom. After all, inclusion is a mindset—not a specific location.

Through this book, it is my hope that you feel empowered as an educator to provide the best inclusive education practices, strategies, and interventions for your students with IEPs. I'm excited that you've picked this book up to read and study because that shows your dedication to your students. They might not tell you so, but you are an amazing educator, and I see your passion for reaching and teaching all students in your classroom. Thank you for believing in the power of inclusive education.

—Rebekah Poe, M. Ed.

ACRONYMS AND TERMS
TO KNOW

Accommodations: an alteration of environment, curriculum format, or equipment that allows an individual with a disability to gain access to content and/or complete assigned tasks

ADHD: Attention Deficit Hyperactivity Disorder

Appropriate Evaluation: students are entitled to have their academic progress and behavior evaluated with tests and observation by trained and qualified individuals

ASD: Autism spectrum disorder

BIP: a written improvement plan created for a student based on the outcome of the functional behavior assessment (FBA)

Eligibility: for a student to be found eligible for special education , the child must fall under one of the thirteen disability categories under IDEA and require specially designed instruction to make progress through the curriculum

ED/EBD: Emotional Disorder/Emotional or Behavioral Disorder

DD: Developmental Delay

FAPE (Free Appropriate Public Education): a component of the law that requires that school districts provide access to general education and specialized educational services and that children with disabilities receive support free of charge as is provided to non-disabled students

FBA (Functional Behavior Assessment): a process for identifying problem behaviors and developing interventions to improve or eliminate those behaviors

HI: Hearing Impairment

ID: Intellectual Disability

IDEA (Individuals with Disabilities Education Act): a law that makes available a free appropriate public education to eligible children with disabilities throughout the nation and ensures special education and related services to those children

IEP (Individualized Education Plan): an individualized education plan or program developed to ensure that a child with an identified disability who is attending an elementary or secondary educational institution receives specialized instruction and related services

LRE (Least Restrictive Environment): a legal term meaning a child with a disability must be educated within the same classroom as typical mainstreamed non-disabled peers to the fullest extent possible for that child in order to ensure that a child with a disability is receiving a free appropriate public education

Modifications: methods that change what the student is expected to learn

MTSS: a framework that uses data-based problem solving and evidence-based practices to ensure that all students receive the support they need to succeed. MTSS is a preventative approach that aims to meet students' academic, behavioral, and social-emotional needs

OHI: Other Health Impairment

OI: Orthopedic Impairment

OT: Occupational Therapy/Therapist

Parent Participation: a component of IDEA stating schools are required to accommodate parents to ensure their attendance and participation at meetings where their child's special education services are discussed and obtain permissions before any testing or services may begin

PLAAFP (Present levels of academic achievement and functional performance): the section of the IEP that summarizes the student's current level of academic proficiency and functional skills

Procedural Safeguards: a set of requirements that go across the laws and regulations of IDEA to protect the rights of children with disabilities and their families, particularly in regard to the access to free appropriate public education (FAPE) (U.S. Department of Education, n.d.)

Psychometrist: a professional who administers and scores psychological and neuropsychological tests to assess a person's mental and psychological state. They also interpret the results of these tests, integrate other medical information, and write reports

PT: Physical Therapy/Therapist

SLD: Specific Learning Disability

SLP: Speech Language Pathologist

SLI: Speech Language Impairment

TBI: Traumatic Brain Injury

UDL: Universal Design for Learning

VI: Visual Impairment

CHAPTER 1:
LET'S TALK IDEA

HISTORY OF IDEA

Inclusion can be an educational buzzword. A lot of people say it or claim they practice it, but what does it mean beyond the surface level? At its most basic, inclusion means "the state of being included" (Merriam-Webster, 2024). In education, it typically means that students with disabilities are included in the general education classroom. We often see schools and classrooms where students with disabilities are physically present and it's called "inclusion." But is it truly inclusive? Is a student being physically present in a classroom enough for them to feel included and successfully learn?

I'm quite positive I just heard a resounding "no" come from those of you reading this book. Chances are, if you were someone who thought the bare minimum was enough, you wouldn't be reading this book right now. And the fact that you are shows that you want to dive further into what it means to provide a fully inclusive education. So let's get to it!

> **Prior to IDEA, only 20% of students with disabilities received an education.**

The idea of inclusive education goes back to the inception of the Individuals with Disabilities Education Act (IDEA) (U.S. Department of Education, n.d.). Created in 1975 as the Education for all Handicapped Children Act (EHA), this law, for the first time, began to protect the rights of children with disabilities. Prior to this law, only 20% of students with disabilities received an education, with many states having harsh restrictions preventing students with any disabilities or impairments from receiving education in a public school. To put it in perspective, men were able to go to the moon before children with disabilities were allowed to attend school with their nondisabled peers.

EHA was the first step taken to support states in providing for and meeting the needs of families of children with disabilities. In 1990, the law was over-hauled and the name changed to the Individuals with Disabilities Education Act (IDEA) (U.S. Department of Education, n.d.). IDEA updates included explicitly listing eligible disability categories covered under the act and lowered the age that children could receive interventions. This allowed interventions to occur from birth as opposed to having to wait until age three. It also mandated the inclusion of a plan of support for students transitioning from school to post-secondary life. The law has been revised multiple times within the last 30 years to update language around disabilities, increase parental rights, and ensure that students with disabilities receive special education services within the least restrictive environment possible.

Today, IDEA is comprised of six main pillars: Free Appropriate Public Education (FAPE), appropriate evaluation, Individualized Education Plan (IEP), Least Restrictive Environment (LRE), parent participation, and procedural safeguards (U.S. Department of Education, n.d.). Each pillar serves a specific purpose in improving the education and preserving the rights of students with disabilities.

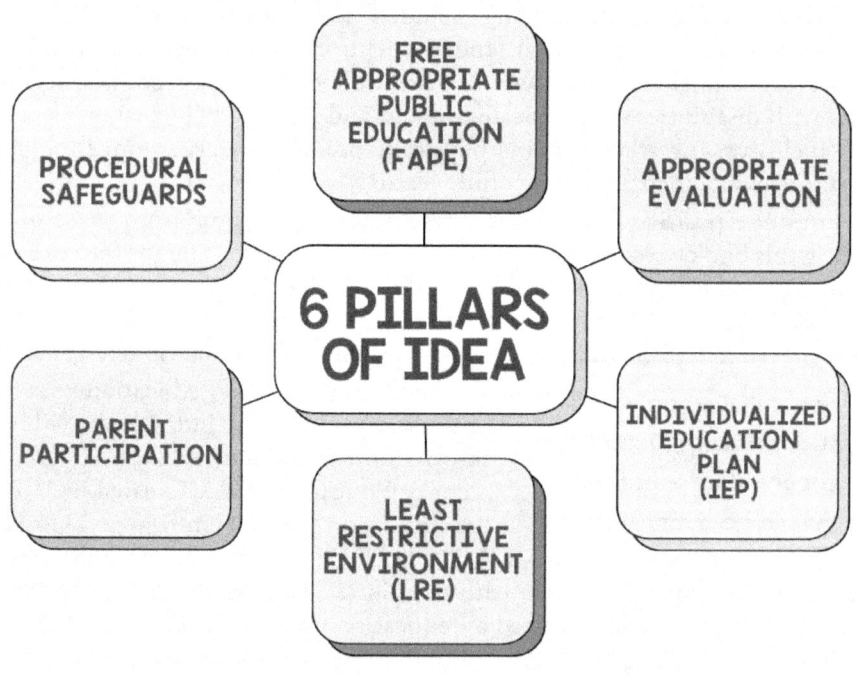

PILLARS OF IDEA

PILLAR 1: FREE APPROPRIATE PUBLIC EDUCATION (FAPE)

Free Appropriate Public Education (or FAPE) is the portion of IDEA that ensures every student, regardless of the severity of their disability, receives free, appropriate public education between the ages of 3 and 21. FAPE is explicitly defined as including:

- Education services that meet the unique educational needs of students with disabilities as adequately as they meet the needs of nondisabled students

- The placement of each student with a disability in the same educational setting, to the maximum extent appropriate, as the student's nondisabled peers

- Appropriate evaluations and placement procedures set up to prevent misclassification or inappropriate placement of students

- Systematic reevaluation of students who have received special education or related services to determine continued qualification

For an education to meet the unique needs of students with disabilities, it must be individually designed based on the needs of each specific child. That is where a student's Individualized Education Program/Plan (IEP) comes in. The IEP outlines a student's educational goals for the school year, lists necessary accommodations and/or modifications, and related services, in addition to other prevalent information pertaining to the student's education that we will cover in a later section.

As a part of FAPE, everything within the IEP must be provided to the student and their family at no cost to the family. This can include related services such as occupational or physical therapy, speech and language services, organizational tools, and necessary technology to make the school and the curriculum accessible.

In addition to accessing education, students with disabilities must be educated in the same setting as their nondisabled peers to the greatest extent possible. This varies from student to student, but the goal is to make sure each student can spend as much time as possible receiving their education in the general education classroom—*your classroom*. On the same wavelength, FAPE also ensures that students are not prohibited or disqualified from their participation in an academic or extracurricular setting based on their disability. To summarize FAPE in one sentence: Every student in your classroom has the legal right to be there.

PILLAR 2: APPROPRIATE EVALUATION

The process for evaluating special education students starts with interventions and increasing support in the general education curriculum and setting. If it is determined that insufficient progress has been made, then a student can be considered for an evaluation.

But according to IDEA, the evaluation of the student must make sense for the student to result in a fair representation of their academic achievement or aptitude. Tests must be both age appropriate and developmentally appropriate and should be conducted by qualified professionals. The results must also be interpreted by those with knowledge of how to read the results. Students should never be subjected to unnecessary testing. After the initial evaluation, if it is determined that a student meets the eligibility requirements and is accepted for special education services, the student must be reevaluated, typically within a three-year cycle, to determine continued eligibility.

As part of each evaluation, the general education teacher will likely be asked to complete a series of rating scales that will be scored by a trained evaluator. You will also need to supply data collected during the school year showing a student's level of progress. Each school will have different specifications for this, so follow up with your special education team for clarification.

PILLAR 3: INDIVIDUALIZED EDUCATION PLAN/PROGRAM (IEP)

An Individualized Education Plan/Program or IEP is the guiding document for a student's education after being identified and meeting eligibility requirements for special education. An IEP is made up of seven key components:

- Present levels of academic achievement and functional performance (PLAAFP)
- Challenging, ambitious, and measurable goals
- Description of special education and related services and supplementary services
- The date of service initiation, frequency, duration, location
- Statement of student's participation in state and district-wide assessments
- Method for measuring and reporting progress
- Explanation of the extent the student will not be educated with non-disabled students in the general education setting (IrisCenter, 2024)

These seven key components are too crucial to just glaze over. Let's take a deeper look. First, we'll dive into the present levels of academic achievement and functional performance, also known as the PLAAFP. The PLAAFP is the section of the IEP that summarizes the student's current level of academic proficiency and functional skills. It includes their strengths along with how the student's disability plays a role in their involvement or lack thereof in the classroom. The PLAAFP is the baseline that will aid in the creation of academic, social, behavioral, and/or functional goals as part of the student's IEP, in addition to shaping accommodations and services required for the student to be able to meet those goals.

The next part of the IEP is the goals. While the goals themselves must be individualized based on the PLAAFP and the needs of the student, they have specific requirements to meet. First, they need to be relevant to the student's education or access to education meaning that they must help a student progress academically. And academic goals must show how they tie into the grade level general education standards the student is working toward mastering. Goals should help bridge the gap between the student's current level of proficiency and their expected level.

Second, the goals must be measurable. To track progress, the teacher must be able to collect data about it. This means it should have objective, observable outcomes. During the creation of the goal, the IEP team must consider how quantifiable data will be collected, whether through teacher observation, grades, trials, or some other way. Goals should also include the conditions under which it will be measured, the targeted behavior (what you are measuring), the performance criteria (what is expected of the student), and the time frame (usually a school or calendar year).

The third part of the IEP is Special Education, Related, and Supplementary Services. This includes the services that the special education teacher provides students to support them in meeting their IEP goals. It outlines what type of instructional services the special education teacher will provide, in addition to the duration and frequency of each. Related services enable students to benefit from special education resources. These can include speech/language therapy, occupational and/or physical therapy, psychological services, and more. The IEP will also cover the students' participation in state assessments and any supports they will need to do so.

Program accommodations and modifications are also included in this area. While similar, the two terms do not mean the same thing and cannot be used interchangeably. Program accommodations change the way material is accessed. They do not make changes to the expected learning material, nor do they lessen the requirements. Accommodations might include extended time to complete a task, material read aloud to a student, or the use of manipulatives. Modifications, however, are changes to the material itself. With modifications, the curriculum is fundamentally altered, either in content or in expectations.

In addition to goals and services, the IEP addresses measuring student progress. It dictates how progress will be monitored and how often it will be done. It also covers the parameters for mastery, and how often progress reports will be made available to families. The first step to creating a process for progress monitoring is to decide how it will be measured. It must be done in an observable, objective manner. Work samples, test scores, and behavior observation checklists are some examples of different types of data that can be used to measure student progress.

Second, the plan must cover how often data will be collected to be used for progress monitoring. It will be determined by the type of skill or goal. Something academic might be conducted weekly and collected as a test score. Something behavioral might be more frequent based on how often the behavior occurs. As for mastery, the progress monitoring plan will state what the minimum score should be and how many occurrences of that score need to occur for the goal to be considered mastered. Parents, as members of the IEP team, have a right to frequent feedback regarding their students' progress, and regular reports should be given to keep families updated. Generally, I typically send progress reports out at the end of every 9 weeks, just like a report card.

The next portion of the IEP delves into a justification for why a student might ***not*** receive all special education services with nondisabled peers, which leads us into the next pillar.

PILLAR 4: LEAST RESTRICTIVE ENVIRONMENT OR LRE

One main component of IDEA is that students are educated to the maximum extent appropriate with their nondisabled peers. The setting in which a student's education takes place is therefore referred to as the Least Restrictive Environment (LRE). It is the location that ensures the student has the greatest chance for academic success when receiving specially designed instruction without unnecessarily limiting access to the general education classroom and their nondisabled peers. And just like each student's IEP will not be the same, each student's LRE will not be the same. There is a continuum of least restrictive to most restrictive, starting with the general education classroom (least restrictive) and ending with a hospital setting or residential facility (most restrictive). For students enrolled in a typical school, the LRE can fall somewhere between general education and special education classrooms based on the percentage of the day where the student spends most of their time (the general education classroom or the special education classroom).

A student's LRE should be based on the answer to the following question: "Is the student able to be successful with special education and related services provided in this setting, with accommodations and modifications supplied as needed?" Students should only be removed from the general education environment if they genuinely require it, and then, it should be done as minimally as possible. As I mentioned before, every student in your classroom has the legal right to be there and to learn from you.

A student's LRE can also change with time. In 2016, I taught in a self-contained classroom at a local elementary school. Because not every school in the area offered a self-contained classroom, some students from outside of the school zone were enrolled in my class, one of whom was a sweetheart of a boy who we'll call Juan. He was a first grader with autism who required a significant level of support at school. The lead classroom teacher and I worked with him and saw him improve by leaps and bounds in both academic and social skills.

The next school year, as a second grader, he began to spend more and more time in the general education classroom. Juan's teacher was so patient with him and viewed him as an equal member in her classroom. By the end of the year, Juan's IEP team felt confident that he would be able to succeed in the general education classroom as his LRE, and he would continue to receive special education services within a small group setting in the resource classroom.

His third-grade year, we both left the self-contained classroom. Juan entered a general education third grade class, and I transferred positions to be the resource and inclusion teacher. He spent most of his day in the general education classroom with an absolute angel of a teacher who was excited to have him in her room. He just visited my resource room once a day for IEP goal instruction. Eventually, the IEP team determined Juan had made such tremendous progress that he was able to transition to the school where he was zoned, because he no longer required a more restrictive environment.

This was not simply a result of any single person's effort. His entire team of teachers and therapists were willing to work together and see Juan as our student. We were able to provide him the opportunity to learn and grow to the greatest extent possible. His family was also highly involved in the entire process, which leads me to the next pillar—Parent Participation.

PILLAR 5: PARENT PARTICIPATION

In my state, at the beginning of every meeting, we have to make sure all members of the meeting sign a record of access, meaning that everyone who signs has accessed and reviewed the student's records. On this document, there is also a number assigned to each category of attendee, from parent to teacher and everyone in between. On this document, the parent (or the student's family member) is listed as number one. I always told my parents in meetings that they were the number one most important part of the IEP meeting (other than their student) because without the parent's permission, nothing could happen. This typically helped to put parents and families at ease. It's common for them to feel like their student receiving an IEP is something that happens *to* them—not something that happens *with* them. Explaining how valuable their participation is helps them to know that we the teachers are on the same side as they are—wanting to provide their student with the greatest opportunity for success. Parent participation is not just encouraged, it is part of the federal law pertaining to special education. So what exactly does that look like?

The school does everything it can to ensure that the parent of the student is able to be present at meetings. This means sending multiple invitations (in writing) early enough for the family to make necessary arrangements to attend. It means trying to schedule the meeting at a time that is convenient for everyone to attend. The parents are made aware of every other person who is invited to the meeting. Additionally, they must be given a copy of the IEP and a copy of their special education rights. Parents must also give permission for services to be carried out, for changes to be made to their child's IEP, and for any special education testing to occur.

On occasion, it may so happen that families are not involved in the development of a student's IEP and a meeting may be held without them. This can happen for a variety of reasons, and when it does, it is essential to have records of the invitations sent and attempts made to get their participation. This leads us to pillar 6—Procedural Safeguards.

PILLAR 6: PROCEDURAL SAFEGUARDS

Procedural safeguards include a copy of the Special Education Rights under IDEA that is given to families as a part of their special education journey. This document provides explanations regarding parental involvement, independent evaluations, mediation and due process hearings, as well as parental consent, student placement, actions, appeals, and attorney fees. A copy is typically given at the onset of a student being referred for special education testing. It's also handed out annually at the student's IEP meeting, or by parent request.

Each of these pillars is equally important when it comes to ensuring that teachers are meeting the requirements of IDEA. The pillars form a comprehensive framework for fostering an environment where every individual can thrive. They promote accessibility, awareness, and accountability for all members of the educational team.

CHAPTER 2:
SPECIAL EDUCATION ELIGIBILITY

Okay, wow. I know that was a lot. Go grab a cup of coffee or can of soda (I prefer Diet Dr. Pepper), and we'll do a virtual, long-distance *cheers* to congratulate you on making it this far.

Understanding the framework for IDEA is your first step in increasing your ability to provide inclusive education, but the first step for your students is determining eligibility.

I have sat in on multiple meetings where teachers are reviewing data to determine if sufficient progress was being made. I have seen teachers pouring everything they can into their students and still not seeing the level of success they knew those students were capable of. When that occurred, it was time for us to start to look at the requirements to determine if the student may be eligible for special education services.

I know there have been students you've seen before who you are just *sure* would benefit from special education services. But the eligibility process is just that—a process. And you as the general education teacher play a large role!

THE REFERRAL PROCESS

I remember several years ago when a second-grade student at an area school had seemingly hit a plateau when it came to his math skills. Despite his best efforts and intervention from his teacher, he still seemed stuck. However, when it came to his reading ability, he was making progress consistently. His teacher began to wonder if his struggle in math was more than a lack of understanding and instead perhaps a disability. At a data meeting where we all came together to review the student's progress, we decided to begin the process to see if he might in fact be eligible for special education services. We decided to submit a request for a referral, the first step in the eligibility process.

A request for a referral can come from either the school or the parent. In my home state of Alabama, a written request for a referral initiates the eligibility process, which must be completed within 90 days. Once a request has come in, a special education teacher typically begins collecting all the necessary documentation—and I do mean *all*.

As part of the referral process, other considerations for why a student might be unsuccessful in the classroom must be examined. These considerations can include:

- Environmental or Economic Concerns:
    o Has the child had limited access to educational experiences (a head start program, preschool, etc.)?
    o Has the child had limited school attendance?
    o Has the child changed schools multiple times?
    o Has the child had home responsibilities that have interfered with learning?

- Linguistic Concerns:
    o Is there a lack of proficiency in the child's language?
    o Is another language spoken in the home that is different from the language used in the school setting that is creating a barrier to their learning?
    o Has there been limited opportunity for them to acquire depth in the English language?

- Cultural Concerns:
    o Are there cultural differences that might be impacting the way the student is perceived by the teacher (verbal and nonverbal communication, social cues, eye contact, etc.)?

These concerns play a role in how the child has been accessing educational material and also in the types of materials and evaluations that they might need for special education testing.

In addition to external concerns, there is another area that must be addressed. To what extent have the current classroom interventions impacted the student's academic performance? Typically, six to nine weeks of documentation is beneficial for providing a comprehensive look at a child's progress. The data collected over the course of those weeks is usually enough to determine if an intervention has been successful or not.

This is where you come in as the general education teacher. You will be asked to show data regarding what interventions you've tried in your classroom (pre-teaching, reteaching, small group instruction, an intervention curriculum, etc.) as well as the results of those interventions—such as work samples and grades.

You will also have to show that the student has participated in a research-based reading and/or math curriculum and received standards-based instruction from a highly qualified teacher. Without proper documentation, it can be very difficult to prove that a student has received everything needed within the classroom to show that special education testing is the next proper step. And that doesn't go just for academic concerns. The same applies for behavioral referrals, as well.

What behavior interventions have you been doing in the classroom and to what extent have they been effective in reducing or alleviating the negative or problematic behavior? Without classroom interventions, in academics or behavior, there will likely be insufficient data to justify special education testing. So your job in taking and presenting that data is essential.

After reviewing the data, the referral for special education testing may either be accepted or rejected. If the referral is rejected, you can still continue collecting data on the student's progress and providing the interventions that were working to support them. If the referral is accepted, that does not guarantee eligibility. Rather, it means that the student is going to be evaluated to determine if they are eligible to receive special education services.

That's a very important difference. I've had general education teachers and parents assume that once the referral was accepted that the student would be in special education. That's why it is so important to understand the process—so you know it for yourself, but also so you can help explain it to a parent or family member who is less familiar with education.

EVALUATION FOR ELIGIBILITY

So the student's referral is accepted: now what? Well, part of your job is already done. Thanks to your data and insight into your student, you are ready for the next step. Your student's IEP team will thank you!

The data you submitted for the referral will be used as part of the student's eligibility. The special education teacher or counselor or whomever is handling the referral may need more information from you.

At this point, someone trained in giving the evaluations will determine the type of evaluation given to the student, will test them, and will interpret the results of those evaluations. The type of evaluation given is determined by the suspected area of disability, and not every area of disability falls under IDEA.

For a student to be deemed eligible for special education, the student must fall into one of 13 disability categories:

- Specific Learning Disability
- Other Health Impairment (such as ADHD, ADD, etc.)
- Speech or Language Impairment

- Autism Spectrum Disorder
- Emotional Disturbance
- Visual Impairment, including Blindness
- Deafness
- Hearing Impairment
- Deaf-Blindness
- Orthopedic Impairment
- Intellectual Disability
- Traumatic Brain Injury
- Multiple Disabilities

Another category where students can be found eligible is "Developmental Delay." However, a child cannot be considered to have a developmental delay past the age of 9. At that time, the child will either be found ineligible or will qualify under a different category. As of 2022 (nces.ed.gov), the breakdown of students with disabilities by disability category was as follows:

Special Education Breakdown by Disability Category	
Specific Learning Disability	32%
Speech Language Impairment	19%
Other Health Impairment	15%
Autism	12%
Developmental Delay	7%
Intellectual Disability	6%
Emotional Disturbance	5%
Multiple Disabilities	2%
Visual Impairment Hearing Impairment Traumatic Brain Injury Deafness Deaf-Blindness Orthopedic Impairment	<2%

Let's take a brief look at characteristics of each of these categories.

SPECIFIC LEARNING DISABILITY

A "Specific Learning Disability" (or SLD) is a disability pertaining to a student's ability to listen, think, read, write, spell, or perform mathematical equations that negatively impacts their ability to progress through the curriculum.

- SLDs can occur in one or more of the following areas:
- Reading comprehension
- Reading skills
- Mathematical reasoning
- Mathematical calculation
- Oral expression
- Written expression
- Listening comprehension

Typically students with an SLD will have a discrepancy between their IQ (and predicted academic achievement score based on their intellectual ability) and their actual academic achievement score that cannot be explained by an intellectual disability, an emotional disturbance, hearing or vision problems, or other health impairments.

In the state of Alabama, any child whose actual academic achievement score is lower than their predicted achievement score by 16 or more points in any of the tested areas can potentially be found eligible for special education under the category of specific learning disability. The criteria varies by state, so you will need to discuss with your IEP/special education team what the parameters are for your area. Of the students receiving special education services in the United States during the 2021-2022 school year, over one-third of the students fell into this disability category.

OTHER HEALTH IMPAIRMENT

"Other Health Impairment" (OHI) might sound confusing as a category of disability because what qualifies as "other?" IDEA defines OHI as

> "having limited strength, vitality, or alertness, including a heightened alertness to environmental stimuli, that results in limited alertness with respect to the educational environment, that—
>
> (i) Is due to chronic or acute health problems such as asthma, attention deficit disorder or attention deficit hyperactivity disorder, diabetes, epilepsy, a heart condition, hemophilia, lead poisoning, leukemia, nephritis, rheumatic fever, sickle cell anemia, and To-

urette syndrome; and

(ii) Adversely affects a child's educational performance" (IDEA Sec. 300.8 (c) (9))

Essentially, a student can fall under the OHI disability category if the student has a health problem that negatively impacts their ability to access the educational environment, such as ADHD or Tourette syndrome, which leads to an inability to progress through the general education curriculum. Typically for a student to qualify for OHI, the student will need to submit medical records regarding the condition (if applicable), an impact statement stating how their condition is negatively impacting their educational performance, rating scales that score the way a student's condition is impeding their education, and documentation of interventions and accommodations they have received prior to the referral.

SPEECH AND LANGUAGE IMPAIRMENT

Speech and Language Impairment (SLI) is the second largest disability category with almost 1 in 5 students who receive special education services falling into this category. A speech and language impairment will be a disability affecting a student's speech (articulation, stuttering, pronunciation, etc.), their language (expressive or receptive), or both areas that negatively impacts the student's ability to progress through or participate in the general education curriculum or classroom.

Typically, students being referred for special education testing for SLI will be evaluated by a Speech Language Pathologist (SLP). The SLP can test for issues related to their articulation, vocal quality (pitch, volume, etc.), fluency, and their ability to use and comprehend spoken language. Some students may have errors within their speech that are considered developmentally appropriate, and as such they would not qualify for special education services under IDEA.

Additionally, if the student does have a speech concern, but it is not impeding their educational performance to the point that they require specially designed instruction, then they will not be found eligible for special education services. These students, however, should continue to be monitored as they age (for developmentally appropriate errors) or as they move through the curriculum.

AUTISM

In 2023, the Center for Disease Control released new findings reporting an increase in the prevalence of autism in children from 1 in 44 in 2018 to 1 in 36.

With an increase in population, teachers can be pretty sure that there will be an increase in their classrooms, as well. The CDC defines autism as "a developmental disability that can cause significant social, communication and behavioral challenges" (CDC.gov, 2024). Symptoms of autism can include difficulties in social communication and interaction, repetitive behaviors and interests, and possibly delayed language, cognitive, and/or learning skills.

Autism is a wide spectrum with varying levels of need. According to the *Diagnostic and Statistical Manual of Mental Disorders (DSM-5)*, "doctors categorize autism by assigning level 1, 2, or 3 to two areas of functioning: social communication and restricted, repetitive behaviors" (Legg, 2024).

Level 1 is classified as "requiring support." Individuals at this level may struggle with social interactions and making friends, need help with organization and planning, or have difficulty coping with change.

Level 2 is classified as "requiring substantial support." Those with a level 2 diagnosis may have difficulty expressing themselves and understanding nonverbal communication, such as body language and facial expressions. They may also have difficulty with day-to-day functions.

Level 3 is classified as "requiring very substantial support." These individuals may have difficulty with expressive and receptive language, and engage in repetitive behaviors to the extent that it impacts their ability to function. They may become extremely distressed in the face of a change to their routine or schedule.

Some students with a medical diagnosis of autism may require intensive interventions in a separate setting where their needs can be better met. Others may need minimal support that can be provided within the general education classroom. The range of supports needed can vary widely from student to student.

However, a medical diagnosis of autism does not automatically qualify a student for special education. Students being referred for special education due to autism will be evaluated in the categories of language, intellect, achievement, behavior/adaptive behavior, and rating scales indicating the presence of autism. The issues related to autism must be adversely affecting their educational performance. If a student has autism yet is not deemed eligible for special education, accommodations may still be provided under section 504 of the Americans with Disabilities Act.

EMOTIONAL DISTURBANCE

An emotional disturbance is a condition characterized by an inability to develop or maintain appropriate interpersonal relationships that adversely affects a student's ability for academic and/or social success.

For an emotional disturbance to qualify under IDEA (Sec. 300.8 (c) (4)), it must cause one or more of the following to occur:

- An inability to learn that cannot be explained by intellectual, sensory, or health factors.

- An inability to build or maintain satisfactory interpersonal relationships with peers and teachers.

- Inappropriate types of behavior or feelings under normal circumstances.

- A general pervasive mood of unhappiness or depression.

- A tendency to develop physical symptoms or fears associated with personal or school problems.

To determine eligibility, the special education teacher and/or psychometrist will likely need you as the student's general education teacher to complete a behavior rating scale. Additionally, you'll need to participate in an interview to determine to what extent the students' maladaptive behavior is impeding their performance in the classroom.

> **It is essential to keep personal feelings and biases out of the evaluation process.**

When relaying this type of information, it is vital to stick to the observable behavior of the student. In other words, who was involved, what happened, where did it happen, and when did it happen? As difficult as it can sometimes be, it is essential to keep personal feelings and biases out of the evaluation process.

VISUAL IMPAIRMENT, INCLUDING BLINDNESS

To qualify for a visual impairment under IDEA, the student must have a disturbance to their vision that negatively affects their academic performance, even with corrective measures. These conditions may be optometric (dealing with more vision-related concerns) or ophthalmic (related to eye health). Regardless, clinical evaluations by an optometrist or ophthalmologist are required. Additionally, classroom data is needed demonstrating academic problems persisting even after the implementation of accommodations and interventions.

HEARING IMPAIRMENT AND DEAFNESS

It is important to note that hearing impairment and deafness are not the same disability category under IDEA. A hearing impairment is defined as an issue with a student's hearing (permanent or fluctuating) that negatively impacts their educational performance.

Deafness occurs when the hearing loss is so severe that the student is unable to process linguistic information, with or without amplification, to the degree that it negatively affects their educational performance. An audiologist will be involved in the evaluation for a student being considered for either of these categories. Additionally, to qualify, there must be a lack of adequate progress made in the general education curriculum and/or classroom that is directly related to the student's hearing impairment or deafness.

For example, a student whose hearing loss impacts areas such as reading comprehension, auditory processing tasks, or language development may be deemed eligible for special education services. Additionally, a student whose hearing loss impacts their ability to participate fully in the general education classroom, such as in discussions or group activities, to the extent of their non-disabled peers, may be eligible for special education services.

DEAF-BLINDNESS

Deaf-Blindness is an eligibility category in which the student has *both* deafness and blindness where both areas are so severely impaired that no one specific program for either is able to meet their needs. Both audiological and optometric or ophthalmic evaluations must show significant impairment in both areas. Also, the student must demonstrate significant communication difficulties that impede them from making progress through the academic curriculum and participating in the classroom, even after accommodations.

ORTHOPEDIC IMPAIRMENT

An orthopedic impairment is a physical disability related to bone, joint, muscle, or any part of the musculoskeletal system that impedes a student's educational progress and daily functioning. Common conditions that fall into this category can include spina bifida, cerebral palsy, limb difference, congenital anomaly, and more. They can be conditions a student was born with or acquired.

As with other disability categories, a medical diagnosis of an orthopedic impairment is not enough to qualify a student for special education. The condition must have a direct relation to the student's inability to make academic progress even after providing accommodations.

INTELLECTUAL DISABILITY

Eligibility under the category Intellectual Disability is twofold: first, a student must have an intellectual capacity that is significantly below average—typically an IQ score of 70 and below.

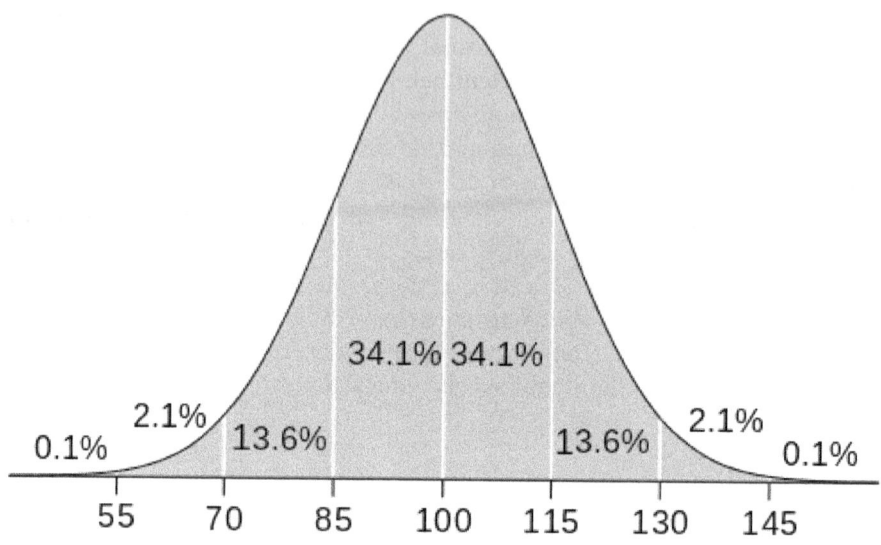

34.1% 34.1%

2.1%

0.1%   13.6%   13.6%   2.1%   0.1%

55   70   85   100   115   130   145

Image from https://sineadaharold.com/2018/08/04/iq-part-1/

The image shown above is called a bell curve. If every single person was represented on this chart, the IQs of the vast majority would fall between 70 and 130. The exact middle is an IQ score of 100. For students with an intellectual disability, their IQs fall into the far-left zones of 70 and below. Individuals with scores of 70 and below are considered to have a significant impairment in their intellectual capacity, meaning in their ability to think through, reason, understand, and process information.

Second, the student must also have issues with adaptive behavior. The American Association of Intellectual and Developmental Disabilities defines adaptive behavior as "the collection of conceptual, social, and practical skills that all people learn in order to function in their daily lives." Where intellect refers to the capacity to learn, adaptive behaviors refers to "learned behaviors that reflect an individual's social and practical competence to meet the demands of everyday living" (aaidd.org, 2024).

Adaptive behavior covers three areas: conceptual skills, social skills, and practical skills. Conceptual skills include reading, math reasoning and computation, etc. Social skills are the interpersonal skills everyone needs to work, interact, and communicate with others. It's how people follow rules, and keep themselves safe from being taken advantage of. Practical skills are the daily living skills an individual must possess to live and function independently. It includes health and hygiene, spending and saving money, etc. An impairment in these types of skills usually means that the individual will require additional supports compared to someone without an intellectual impairment.

These two scores (intellectual and adaptive) are used as part of the eligibility process for special education. A psychometrist or someone else trained in conducting and scoring these tests will evaluate the student. As the general education teacher, you will likely be asked to complete an adaptive behavior rating scale to determine how your student's adaptive functioning impacts their ability to participate in the school environment. Again, it is important to provide honest, fact-based answers to ensure you have represented them as accurately as possible.

TRAUMATIC BRAIN INJURY

A Traumatic Brain Injury (TBI) is an injury sustained by an external force that damages the brain so significantly that educational or functional performance is impeded from progressing in the typical way. A TBI does not include injuries to the brain that occurred during pregnancy or birth or that are caused by congenital or degenerative defects.

To be eligible for the TBI category, there must be medical documentation of the injury along with evidence that the injury has caused an impairment in one or more of the following areas:

- Cognition: the process of acquiring knowledge and understanding
- Language: the ability to communicate and understand communication
- Memory: the faculty by which the mind stores and remembers information
- Attention: notice taken of someone or something
- Reasoning: the action of thinking about something in a logical, sensible way
- Abstract thinking: the ability to consider ideas, principles, and objects that aren't physically present
- Judgment: the ability to make considered decisions or come to sensible conclusions
- Problem-solving: the process of finding solutions to difficult or complex issues
- Sensory: relating to sensation or the physical senses
- Perceptual and motor abilities: a combination of sensory skills and motor skills that allow people to interact with their environment
- Psychosocial behavior: the relation between social influences and in-

dividual psychology

- Physical functions: the ability to perform basic and instrumental activities of daily living

- Information processing: the acquisition, recording, organization, retrieval, display, and dissemination of information

- Speech: the expression of or the ability to express thoughts and feelings by articulate sounds

MULTIPLE DISABILITIES

On occasion, a student may meet eligibility requirements for more than one category under IDEA. If accommodations and interventions in one disability area alone are not enough to meet the student's educational needs, the student may fall under the eligibility category of "multiple disabilities" (note: Deaf-Blindness is its own category and as such does not fall into the realm of "multiple disabilities").

To determine eligibility, students are required to have medical diagnoses (if applicable), evaluations by trained professionals, developmental history, assessment of intellectual and adaptive capacity, and possibly assessments in speech/language, motor skills, and others. Typically, students who fall into this category will require substantially more support across all areas: adaptive, educational, functional, and more. Even when requiring more services, access to an inclusive education is important for the development of social skills and friendships.

UNDERSTANDING STUDENTS WITH IEPS

Each of the above disabilities make a student eligible for special education services. As we read, the representation of each of these disabilities can vary from more prevalent to not very prevalent at all. We can divide these disabilities into three categories: high incidence, medium incidence, and low incidence.

HIGH INCIDENCE DISABILITIES

High incidence disabilities are the disabilities that affect the greatest number of individuals and as such are more prevalent in schools and classrooms. High incidence disabilities may include:

- Specific Learning Disability

- Speech Language Impairment

- Other Health Impairment (ADHD, etc.)

Students with these types of disabilities are usually able to participate to a great extent if not fully within the general education classroom. They just require a little more support—such as accommodations, unique learning models, and special education services to help bridge any gaps. Academically, students with high-incidence disabilities may struggle with specific subjects, such as reading and mathematics. Some may struggle with language and communication skills, and others may struggle with executive functioning or all the above.

Students with high incidence disabilities can receive much of their instruction within the general education classroom with collaboration between general education and special education teachers. This teamwork ensures that the IEP is in place and being followed and that the students are receiving the accommodations and services they need to make progress in the general education curriculum.

MEDIUM INCIDENCE DISABILITIES

Medium incidence disabilities are the ones that are somewhat prevalent. Students with these disabilities might receive services either within the general education classroom or in a special education classroom. They may also alternate settings depending on their level of need.

Medium instance disabilities include:

- Autism Spectrum Disorder
- Developmental Delay
- Intellectual Disability
- Emotional Disturbance

Students with these disabilities might struggle academically, linguistically, socially, emotionally, and/or cognitively. These disabilities do not occur as often as high incidence disabilities, however a general education teacher might have students with these disabilities in the general education classroom. They might be in the classroom for the majority of the day or they might come in just for an hour or so. The disabilities that fall into this category might require students to have more supports put in place than their high incidence counterparts, but that does not mean that inclusive education is out of their reach. With the right tools and accommodations in place, an inclusive environment can work well to meet the needs of each of these students.

Something to be aware of is that while both are still considered to be in the medium incidence category, diagnoses of autism and developmental delay have increased over the last few years. In fact, some documents are beginning to include autism in the high incidence category.

Additionally, developmental delay can only be applied to students under the age of nine. To continue to qualify for special education services past that age, the student must be identified under another disability category—typically SLD, SLI, or ID.

LOW INCIDENCE DISABILITIES

Low incidence disabilities are the disabilities that make up the smallest percentage of students who receive special education services. Only about 2-3% of the student population will fall into one of these categories.

Low incidence disabilities include:

- Multiple Disabilities
- Visual Impairment
- Hearing Impairment
- Traumatic Brain Injury
- Deafness
- Deaf-Blindness
- Orthopedic Impairment

For some of these disabilities, students will require significant assistance and support. Others might need only a few accommodations. It is important to know that low incidence does *not* mean "low functioning" (a term I *despise*). As with all disability categories, there can be a wide level of need as no two students, even with the same disabilities, have the same needs.

> **No two students, even with the same disabilities, have the same needs.**

In my career, I taught in a wide variety of classrooms: everything from full inclusion to entirely separate self-contained settings. My students ran the gamut—from specific learning disabilities to multiple disabilities. Their needs were different which meant the support I provided was different. But one thing was the same no matter where I was teaching: each of my students deserved the opportunity to learn in the way that worked the best for them. Each of my students deserved to feel like they belonged. Each deserved to feel included.

I may have been the special education teacher, but this large task was not something I could achieve on my own. True change requires everyone believing that an inclusive education is not only what a student deserves, but also that it is what is best for everyone, whether they have disabilities or not.

CHAPTER 3:
DEFINING INCLUSIVE EDUCATION AND ITS BENEFITS

The concept of a more inclusive education has been around for about 50 years. It started with the development of the Education for All Handicapped Children Act in 1975 and developed more with the advent of IDEA in 1990. Over the years, as more and more schools have embraced inclusive education and more and more students have had access to education in their Least Restrictive Setting (LRE), we have seen an abundance of benefits, not only to students receiving special education services but also to their nondisabled counterparts.

When I worked at the high school level, I accompanied two students with moderate disabilities (with LREs of the self-contained classroom) to their elective, general education art classes. While I was there to provide support if needed, the students did not actually need me at all.

In art, they sat at tables with typical peers and talked and laughed right along with them while working on their art projects. With difficult projects, such as weaving, their newfound friends were patient to help them with intricate strings that wound over and under in repeating patterns. Their completed projects were displayed alongside the others, with all students excited to show off their designs. And I got to enjoy watching a group of teenagers interact with one another as friends regardless of any perceived differences.

BENEFITS TO STUDENTS IN SPECIAL EDUCATION

PEER ROLE MODELS

Personally, I saw both my students with disabilities and their nondisabled peers grow not only academically, but also socially while participating in an inclusive classroom. For my students with disabilities, I saw improvements in the classroom ranging from increasing their test scores to meeting their IEP goals and improving their communication skills.

In 2019, I had a student who we'll call Camilla. She was the sweetest second grader in the world, but she was significantly behind her typical peers in terms of speech, reading fluency, and mathematical reasoning. I remember all of her teachers being extremely concerned because she was having such a difficult time making any progress. It was like one step forward and two steps back. We had a very tough, honest decision about whether receiving most of her instruction in the general education classroom was actually what was best for her academically. Her tests and evaluations were borderline, and really, she could have gone either way.

We eventually decided to keep her in the same LRE (least restrictive environment) she'd been in—with her still spending most of the day in the general education classroom. But we increased the time she spent in my resource special education classroom for small group instruction for reading and math. We did this for a couple of different reasons.

First, Camilla loved her friends in her class. She had known some of them since kindergarten. They knew her, and loved her, too. Being surrounded by her nondisabled peers benefited Camilla because she got to experience friendship in a real way. She went to PE and recess with them. She sat with them in the library and at lunch. If we had changed her LRE and placed her in the more restrictive setting, would she still be able to cultivate those friendships? Possibly, but not likely at the same level. It would have hurt her to be taken from the class she knew and loved. The negatives outweighed the positives when it came to moving Camilla.

Second, it wasn't just that she had friends; it was that with those friends, she had peer models, helpers, and leaders. As I mentioned, Camilla had a significant speech impairment. It sometimes took even familiar listeners a couple of attempts before we could understand what she was saying. Within the general education classroom, Camilla was able to participate in natural, free-flowing conversation with her friends. She heard appropriate speech being used and modeled for her, which research shows can have a significant impact on influencing language growth. Being surrounded by and talking with her friends wasn't just a fun activity—it was helping her improve her communication ability.

Finally, her friends made amazing peer tutors. The group Camilla surrounded herself with was so open to helping her and did so with kindness. I truly applaud that teacher for creating such a welcoming, inviting classroom where everyone treated each other with compassion. It allowed for some wonderful experiences for Camilla and other students like her in the classroom. Her teacher would pair or group students together to work on assignments—always strategically. Camilla would be placed with students who were willing to help, who had a good grip on the concept of the assignment, and who would be able to not only help her, but also make sure she felt like a true member of their group. Sometimes, after teaching a new concept, Camilla would gain a better understanding after working with her group than she got just from the instruction from the teacher.

There have been times I've even been like that. I've listened to someone trying to teach me something, but not really understood it until a peer explained it to me in familiar terms that made more sense. It happens with our students, too. And it warms this teacher's heart to watch students come together to learn something new.

These stories are great, but they aren't just stories. They're evidence that inclusive education really is beneficial to students in special education. They aren't just my stories either. There are stories just like this from around the globe that are cited in research and reports repeatedly proving the benefits of inclusive education—but when they're in research and reports, they're called "case studies."

LANGUAGE AND COMMUNICATION

A study was published in 2020 showing how the language growth of preschool students with disabilities was directly impacted by the language development of their nondisabled peers. As you'll remember, language impairments do not just refer to spoken language or speech, but also expressive and receptive communication (including listening comprehension). The research showed that students who had regular and repeated interactions with their nondisabled peers within an educational environment had a greater improvement in their communication and language skills than students who did not have those interactions (Chen, et al., 2020).

Another study in 2016 involved a group of third graders with significant learning and speech disabilities, much like my sweet Camilla. During the study, students were tasked with writing short stories that followed a simple, three-part structure with a "beginning, middle, ending" sequence. This is important because writing requires a lot of skills: mental processing, sequencing, language, communication, motor skills, and more. As expected, the group of students had a very difficult time with their assignments. On average, the students' first stories were only between 25 and 50 words long. Over the course of the study, they were partnered with higher-performing students for 45 minute "peer tutoring" sessions. Each student pair participated in 5-7 sessions.

The peer tutors showed the students how to use graphic organizers, similar to the one shown below, as part of a "prewriting" process where students plan what they are going to write about. While this portion of the writing process is difficult for students with learning and language disabilities because of the

Pre-Writing: I can plan my story!

Name: **Date:**

Characters:	Setting:

Beginning	Middle	Ending

@RebekahPoeTeaching

mental processing and sequencing involved in planning a narrative, the graphic organizer made a difference. It allowed the students a better way to visualize their story before beginning writing. The peer tutors modeled the "prewriting" phase and the use of the graphic organizers. The pairs chose an essay topic, and the tutors demonstrated their brainstorming processes, thinking out loud about who their characters could be, where their story could take place, and the events that might happen.

After watching the peer tutors, the tutees followed suit, receiving guidance from the tutors as needed. The results improved immediately after only one session and continued to trend upward as the sessions continued. Where the students were initially writing only an average of about 37 words, they ended up writing stories of 124 words on average, an increase of approximately 335%! I don't know about you, but 300% growth over the course of seven sessions blows my mind. Working with their peers, these students were able to watch an age-appropriate writing process occur, and then replicate it themselves. As you can see, the benefits of having students with disabilities learn alongside their typical peers are indisputable (Grünke, Janning, & Sperling, 2016).

SOCIAL SKILLS

However, it is not only in language or academics where studies prove the benefits of inclusive education. Other studies have shown how inclusive education has provided positive social interactions. That means it improves social, emotional, and behavior skills, as well. One of the clearest markers of a successful inclusive classroom is the degree to which each student feels like they belong.

> " Having a sense of belonging boosts self-esteem and confidence. It increases motivation. And it is not something that is done by accident. "

Inclusion is not a place; it is a mindset. For a student to truly be included, it is not enough that they are physically present in the classroom, merely being taught alongside their typical peers. They must be a welcomed, accepted, valued member of that classroom who feels comfortable enough to participate, share, and learn.

Having a sense of belonging boosts self-esteem and confidence. It increases motivation. And it is not something that is done by accident. This sense of belonging stems from positive social interactions from student to student. There are more things happening in a classroom than just teaching and learning. There are friendships being made; relationships growing. And for students with both academic and social skills deficits, that can be a negative "double whammy" when it comes to classroom performance. In fact, researchers have speculated that "social skill deficiencies may be as disabling as academic deficits, creating double handicaps for many children with disabilities."

Students who have struggles around appropriate social skills might also have issues showing empathy for others, a lack of impulse control, and a limited ability to come up with appropriate solutions to problems that arise in the classroom. Learning alongside peers who do not have the same social skills deficits allows students with disabilities to observe appropriate social interactions, problem solving processes, and decision-making. It gives them the opportunity to participate in these situations.

As a teacher, I frequently had students on my caseload who had behavioral goals. We discussed the difference between "expected" and "unexpected" behaviors and how they might impact or influence the student's classroom experience. We role-played through different scenarios, which was great practice. However, social skills are best taught and learned when students are able to have these interactions with other students in a safe environment.

In my resource classroom, it occasionally looked like my students were just "playing." But that unstructured time gave my students the opportunity to interact with one another without teacher facilitation. I pulled out board games, paper and markers, and toy cars that they could use and play with on their own.

I loved watching their imaginations take over as they made up rules for games and played pretend with imaginary scenarios. And though it looked like the students were just "playing," they were learning to problem solve, practicing communication, and making friends.

> **When students are taught in an inclusive environment, they tend to have an overall higher level of academic achievement.**

INCREASED ACHIEVEMENT OF IEP GOALS

The benefits of inclusion for students in special education are not limited to improved social skills. When students are taught in an inclusive environment, they tend to have an overall higher level of academic achievement, as well. And as teachers, isn't that our ultimate goal?

A study published in 2021 analyzed and compared the academic progression of students with IEPs who were taught in inclusive classrooms and those who were taught in regular/non-inclusive classrooms. Students who participated in inclusive classrooms saw a greater increase in academic achievement scores compared to those who were not (59.45 vs 55.08) (Kart and Kart, 2021). But why and how does this occur? It starts with the IEP.

STANDARDS-ALIGNED INSTRUCTION

Unless it is stated that the student is working on alternate achievement standards, a student's IEP should have academic goals that are directly aligned to the general education curriculum standards. And where is the general education curriculum being taught but in the general education classrooms? Therefore, it makes sense that in order for students to have the best access to general education standards, they should be receiving instruction in that same classroom, as well.

Students with disabilities need to be challenged when it comes to making academic progress. To that end, students in inclusive classrooms are held to the same standards as their typical peers. They receive accommodations within the classroom, but as we discussed earlier, accommodations do not reduce academic rigor. They just make the curriculum more accessible for students with disabilities. They are still expected to be able to learn the same material and produce the same types of outcomes. There is no lowering of expectations because a student has a disability, and each student is taught the same material.

This is especially important for older students who are earning class credits for graduation. For a diploma, certain standards must be learned. If we lower the expectations and fail to teach them, our students run the risk of not earning the necessary amount of class credits, which can impact the diploma or certificate they receive upon graduation.

Differentiated instruction or co-teaching within the general education inclusive setting makes it easier for students to access those standards much in the same way as their typical peers. It helps them be well on their way to earning a typical high school diploma. With a high school diploma, students have a higher success rate of finding employment or pursuing further education, which is why we must make sure to prioritize it.

However, something else these studies have shown is that the type of inclusive education the students receive plays the largest factor in determining how much academic success students have. Inclusion takes teamwork—from the general education teacher, the special education teacher, and the entire IEP team. When co-teaching in an inclusive setting is implemented with fidelity, students with disabilities can find greater academic success when working alongside their typical peers (Wood, 2019).

INCREASED STAFF COLLABORATION

In a truly inclusive setting, there is typically an increase in staff as well as staff collaboration. For instance, a general education teacher and a special education teacher may teach together, which is how I taught at the middle school level. I co-taught two math and two ELA classes alongside the general education teacher. I was there to help provide differentiated instruction, make accommodations, and pre—or re-teach concepts.

However, I wasn't there solely for the students with IEPs. We (the general education teacher and I) each taught every student. There was no delineation between students with IEPs and those without. There was no "your students" or "my students;" they were all "our students." Occasionally, I pulled a small group of students to a table and provided extra instruction. Sometimes the general education teacher provided the extra instruction while I worked with the rest of the class. That set up ensured that every student saw us as equal teachers who were there to teach every student rather than having a "mine and yours" situation. It took teamwork and an overall attitude of respect to make it work—both for the students and for each other, and in our case, it was entirely worth it.

That can be especially helpful when it comes to creating a student's IEP. We know that IEPs are developed in collaboration with the entire IEP team, including both the general and special education teachers. When both teachers work together, there is a greater overall understanding of what students need to work on. Co-teachers can share findings and contribute ideas about necessary accommodations, IEP goals, present level of performance, and other areas.

As a special education teacher, I was not always well-versed in every single grade level subject standard. I relied on my general education teacher counterparts to be the subject area experts. The general education teachers knew what skills needed to build on one another to support progress from standard to standard. I needed their expert opinion to make sure that the goals I wrote for the students' IEPs made logical sense in the scope and sequence of the curriculum. This ensured that the IEP was developed to promote the greatest chance for student success.

Another benefit of having an increase of staff collaboration is the ability for teachers to monitor students and collect student data. As a special education teacher, I was constantly collecting data to monitor the students' progress on their IEP goals. The general education teachers monitored progress for MTSS or RTI. Having us both in the classroom made it so much simpler because there was someone else there to work with other students while we collected the needed data. And if I missed something, there was another set of eyes available to catch it, and vice versa.

BENEFITS TO STUDENTS IN GENERAL EDUCATION

In researching studies to include in this book, I was pleasantly surprised to find almost as many studies on the benefits of inclusive education for students without disabilities as there have been for students *with* disabilities. And just like the benefits for students with disabilities cover academic and social areas, so do the benefits for their typical counterparts.

INCREASED UNDERSTANDING AND ACCEPTANCE OF DIVERSITY

In my high school special education classrooms, where my students mostly had intellectual disabilities like Down Syndrome, I had students who attended classes with general education students as they were able. Some went to classes like art or music; others attended science classes. There were other times of the day when we had typical peers come into our class as peer helpers or aides.

For all the students without disabilities that worked alongside my students, whether in the general education or the special education classroom, it was one of their favorite classes. It wasn't hard to see why. They learned empathy and went out of their way to include and speak with my students. They were willing to step in, to not just be a "helper" but to be a true friend to students they wouldn't have known otherwise. And they learned that they had more in common with them than they might have originally thought.

I'm not sure if you remember when the Whip/Nae Nae song first debuted, but holy smokes, I sure do. The song had every single one of our high school students in a chokehold. You couldn't walk down the halls without seeing arms flailing and hearing teenage voices singing.

When it was time for pep rallies, naturally that song was used to get students up and moving. And my students were some of the highest energy students in the room. In those moments, there were no "typical peers" or "students with significant disabilities." There were just kids, who were singing, laughing, and dancing together. Watching 1000 teens dancing to their favorite song was a pure joy.

When I taught elementary resource, most of my students had specific learning disabilities (SLDs). They spent most of their days in the general education classroom. I noticed that the differences between typical students and those with SLDs were more subtle than the differences between my students with Down syndrome and their typical peers.

And sometimes kids wouldn't understand why one student got one thing, but another student got something different—such as some students using a fidget tool or leaving the classroom to take a test. That provided the general education teacher and me the opportunity to talk about embracing differences. We talked about how each person needs tools to be as successful as possible, and that those tools wouldn't look the same for every student.

It reminds me of "The Bandage Lesson," an older idea for a lesson that has been going around the internet for several years. It took the world by storm when it went viral on TikTok in 2021. In the lesson, teachers would give each student a bandage and assign them different injuries ranging in severity.

One at a time, each student would come to the front of the room to the teacher and tell the "doctor" what their injury was. After the "exam," the teacher/doctor would give the student a bandage. For some students, getting a bandage for their injury made sense (if they had a paper cut, scrape, etc.). For other students, it didn't make sense at all (for pink eye, a broken arm, etc.).

> **Fair doesn't mean that everyone gets the same thing; it means everyone gets what they need.**

I decided to hop on the bandwagon and try it out. Once we got to the point in the activity where I handed out bandages, my students were always confused. They wanted to know how a bandage was supposed to help a runny nose or something equally as absurd. And I always played ignorant: everyone got the same thing; that's "fair," right? "No!" they would shout and laugh!

This brought us into the next portion of the lesson. I asked students why it didn't work when everyone received the same thing if we were trying to keep things "fair." The answer, of course, is that fair doesn't mean that everyone gets the same thing; it means everyone gets what they need.

I love this activity because it helps open discussion about how students in the classroom all have different needs and different tools that will help them do their best. This can include fidget tools, glasses, speech devices, and anything else that is unique to students in your room.

Will each day be perfect? Will everyone intrinsically understand why some students seem to get things that aren't fair? No. But this activity allows for a teaching moment that helps students learn to embrace diversity and promote inclusion for all.

When students without disabilities are taught in classrooms alongside students with disabilities, they begin to understand that each person is unique and has unique needs. They also learn that these differences are good things and should be celebrated.

GREATER ACADEMIC OUTCOMES

The benefits of inclusive education aren't limited only to students receiving special education services. General education students are also seeing the benefit in schools all over the world. Everyone learns differently, not just students with disabilities. And understanding this truth is a main component of inclusive education. When students without disabilities are taught alongside students with disabilities, they typically receive a more differentiated level of instruction along with additional resources that work best for every student.

Additionally, students can develop a deeper understanding of a concept by helping reteach it to a peer who might not have fully understood it the first time. Being able to explain a concept requires a greater depth of knowledge than being able to recall a concept, which leads to greater retention and application.

OPPORTUNITIES TO MASTER ACTIVITIES BY PRACTICING AND TEACHING OTHERS

Several years ago, I co-taught in a 6th grade math classroom. The class was split—about 50% with IEPs and 50% without. The level of ability in that classroom varied widely. There were students who were still working on single digit multiplication and others who grabbed on to new concepts with ease.

One student who we'll call Carson was able to master a new concept after only a few attempts. He loved being challenged with crazy big numbers and equations that had multiple steps. As his teachers, we encouraged that, finding supplemental materials to push him and stretch his mind. Carson was also one of the kindest souls I've ever known. He understood that other children in the class did not catch on to things as fast as him. Carson understood he could help, and he *wanted* to help.

Carson knew *how* to solve equations. However, he didn't always know *why* it worked the way it did. And he was the type of student who wanted to know *why*. Sometimes after completing his own work, he would ask if he could help a friend, which we always encouraged. And as he was going over a concept with a peer, we could see the lightbulb go on for him, too. He would be explaining how to do something, and suddenly he understood "why" it made sense. That would lead him to be able to apply the same information to other equations and math standards, deepening and expanding his own knowledge as he helped his friend.

And this same type of finding remains relatively consistent across case studies. A study in 2019 that compared academic achievement of students both with and without disabilities who participated in a "peer tutoring" program with those who did not. Across the board, all students involved in peer tutoring increased their academic achievement (whether they had disabilities or not). They benefited on a greater scale than those not involved in tutoring (Algere, et. al., 2019). And get this: it didn't matter whether they were the ones tutoring or being tutored, just that they were a part of it!

ALL STUDENTS' NEEDS ARE BETTER MET

Every teacher—from the first year to the 25-year veteran—knows that no two students are going to learn in the exact same way. And that doesn't just apply to students with IEPs. General education students learn in their own unique ways, as well. In an inclusive classroom, the different types of instruction and resources are usually very evident, and that differentiation isn't only provided to students receiving special education services.

Some people believe that students without disabilities are not challenged enough or do not learn enough in an inclusive environment because they are taught at a "lower" level. I've heard that argument from teachers and people in the community alike, but it stems from a lack of real understanding.

In a 2020 study, researchers analyzed the effects of education in an inclusive classroom on students without disabilities—particularly the academic benefits. After all, if we are arguing that inclusive education is best for students, we need to know that it is truly best for all students—those with and without disabilities. The study showed that not only are there no negative effects of an inclusive learning environment on typical students, but that there is a positive effect with academic achievement scores. There was a greater increase in students taught in an inclusive environment as opposed to those who were not. The author stated, "...the benefits of inclusive education were connected to effective classroom practices characterized by learning interactions, such as cooperative and dialogic learning, peer tutoring, or collaborative problem-solving, which are beneficial for all learners in the classroom" (Roldán, et. al., 2021).

Overall, the benefits for students who are taught in inclusive classrooms are evident in both students with disabilities and those without. Students with disabilities who have meaningful connections and interactions with students without disabilities benefited in the areas of language development, cognitive awareness, and social skills. They also gained an enhanced ability to acquire new skills and even went on to generalize those skills across multiple environments.

And for students without disabilities, the opportunity to learn alongside their peers who receive special education services gave them the chance to expand their own cognitive ability by deepening their understanding of concepts when explaining something to their peers. It also enabled them to partake in the differentiated styles of instruction that are often present in classrooms where special education services take place.

When I taught 3rd grade, I had a group of girls who were all working on improving their multiplication fact fluency. In one of our lessons, we learned to skip count by 3s by counting out loud to the tune of the Macarena while doing the motions. The girls thought it was a blast and learned it very quickly.

I released them back to their class, and later in the day, their third-grade teacher found me. She told me that the girls were so excited about their new dance that they taught the rest of the class. By the end of the day, her entire class was singing and dancing and were all able to skip count by 3 with near 100% accuracy. It was all within a day, all because there was a new way for them to learn that was different from what they typically encountered. And my students were thrilled to be able to teach something to their peers. All of our students were winners that day.

CHAPTER 4:
MOTIVATING RELUCTANT LEARNERS

Perhaps you find yourself convinced of the need for an inclusive classroom, but you're not sure how to incorporate it. Let's talk about how you can create an inclusive environment where your students receive the services and education they need to thrive by establishing a positive and supportive classroom culture.

As the saying goes, "You can lead a horse to water but you can't make them drink." I don't know where it originated; I don't remember the first time I heard it. But I definitely remember when I really started to grasp the true meaning of the quote.

My first year *ever* teaching was in 2010 at the ripe old age of 22. I taught art at a private PreK-12 school in North Alabama. I was so excited to get to teach such a wide range of ages and abilities, and I remember having huge plans and ideas for my high schoolers. I was also totally green when it came to my teaching style, so let's just say things weren't the rainbows and sunshine I had envisioned.

I had a student, who we'll call Hal, who was easily the most artistically gifted and talented teenager I'd ever met. He was one hundred times the artist I would ever be. And there he was, sitting in my classroom, bored out of his mind completing assignments I had given to the whole class. Because I was the teacher, I just expected him to do them. But because he was so advanced in his skill, he wasn't interested.

> **If we want students to learn, we need to help them find the motivation!**

Hal and I embarked on a power struggle that lasted for 18 weeks. I demanded he do exactly what was asked of him. Unfortunately, he wanted to do…literally anything else. Looking back now, I can see a teenage boy seeking challenge, seeking connection, seeking autonomy. But at the time, I only saw defiance. My thought was "Why won't he just do what I'm telling him to do? I've given him chance after chance and he refuses!" In other words—I could lead the horse to water, but I couldn't make him drink.

There are a million and one things we're expected to teach students, but they don't have a desire to learn all of it. If we want them to learn, we need to help them find the motivation! And we've all seen how a lack of motivation negatively impacts every aspect of that student's academic career. Grades slip, negative behaviors increase, it can be a distraction to other students, and it can make us feel like we aren't effective teachers. So how can we work toward motivating students to be active participants in their learning?

There are two types of motivation: intrinsic and extrinsic. Intrinsic motivation is "the motivation to engage in a behavior because of the inherent satisfaction of the activity rather than the desire for a reward or specific outcome." Take a couple of moments to think of some tasks that you participate in simply because you enjoy them—not because you get anything tangible out of it. You do those things because of intrinsic motivation.

One example for me is reading. I love absolutely everything about it: scouring the library shelves or my Kindle app, finding just the right book, and finally, losing myself in the story. It's a way for me to escape the real world just for a little bit. And while I enjoy it, there is nothing tangible that I get from reading. I'm not earning money for reading a book (but to be honest, if "professional reader" was a job, I'd take it!). I'm not receiving awards for the number of books read. It's something I do for the sheer pleasure of the experience itself.

The opposite of that is extrinsic motivation, which is "a motivation that is driven by external rewards." The external rewards might be something tangible, like money or a prize, or they might be intangible, like accolades. These might be things we do not enjoy doing, but we must do them for the outcome, or perhaps we do them because of what we will receive once the task is finished.

For example, I find no joy in doing laundry. I doubt I'll ever do it simply because I enjoy it, but I must do it because I can't walk around naked. My motivation for doing laundry is that it would be inappropriate for me to be unclothed or wear dirty clothes.

There can also be tasks that provide both intrinsic and extrinsic motivation, like taking a cooking class. I love trying new recipes—gathering ingredients, combining them in the perfect amount and order. The act of cooking itself can provide me with intrinsic motivation.

However, once the cooking is done—it's time to *eat!* And boy do I love a good meal. I treasure the dishes bursting with flavor that my family adores. That's extrinsic motivation. Regardless of the type, it's the motivation itself that urges us to get stuff done.

Our students are the same way. Motivation plays a key factor in their participation in class, in completing assignments, and in meeting expectations. As a former middle school teacher, there is not a single time I can recall having to tell one of my students, "Hey, you need to play your computer game," or "You need to watch funny YouTube videos." Because those were tasks they actually wanted to do. They were intrinsically motivated to watch YouTube. The videos were fun and kept them entertained.

But do you want to guess how many times I had to tell my students, "Hey, you need to be working on your journal entry," or "You need to finish your math problems"? Whatever number you guessed, multiply it by ten and you are probably halfway to the real answer! Those comments happen way more frequently, because for many students, there isn't a lot of intrinsic motivation to do schoolwork.

This is especially true when it comes to our students with disabilities for whom schoolwork can be more of a struggle. It's much harder to motivate a student in an academic area when they feel like they aren't good at it or like it might be hard. I call this group of students my "reluctant learners."

Reluctant learners are the ones for whom it's going to take just a bit more. I learned that the hard way with Hal. Getting him to buy into what I was teaching was huge! You might have to go a step above to really get them motivated, to get them to participate, and to have them "buy in" to what you're teaching. But it's worth it.

This is especially important when building an inclusive classroom because you are trying to make sure that every student can do just that.

CHAPTER 5:
CREATING AN INCLUSIVE CLASSROOM ENVIRONMENT

When it comes to creating an inclusive classroom, you need to make sure you are implementing four main characteristics into your lessons, student relationships, and classroom environment. You need to show your students that you CARE.

I use the acronym CARE to represent these characteristics because of the old quote "Students won't care how much you know until they know how much you CARE." Students can't learn at maximum capacity if they don't feel safe, if they don't feel like they belong, or if they feel like what is happening doesn't pertain to them. So when we show students we "CARE," we are teaching through a lens of inclusion by focusing on <u>C</u>ollaboration, <u>A</u>uthenticity, <u>R</u>elevance, and <u>E</u>ngagement.

COLLABORATION

Collaboration is not just between teachers like we discussed earlier but includes collaboration between students. And that goes deeper than just assigning students a partner to work with during the day. I mean real collaboration through group work, building a team mindset, and cross-curricular collaboration.

Students doing group work was a game changer for not only student motivation, but also classroom management for me. Students want to be with each other. They want to talk to their friends and sit by their buddies. There's a little bit of that intrinsic motivation we were talking about. The trick is to take that desire and transform it into a teaching tool.

In my teaching journey, I've used some strategies such as turn and talk where they turn to a neighbor and talk about the lesson. I have them summarize what we were talking about with a partner. I have them offer an explanation in their own words of the topic. This way, they're getting that opportunity to talk, but it's controlled. I've also utilized "think, pair, share" where students take a moment to consider their answers to a question and then pair up and share what they've come up with. I've seen so many times where a student who has been struggling with a topic suddenly understands it when another student explains it. Being able to work with a friend or talk with a friend suddenly gives a student extra motivation to participate because they are getting more enjoyment out of the task.

Another idea for collaboration is to encourage that "team mindset" where each student has a role to play and they have to rely on each other to meet a common goal. I've always been the kind of person who, if you give me a job, I'm going to get it done. Likewise, having a job role or a specific responsibility can be remarkably beneficial for some of our students who have potentially problematic attention-seeking or disruptive behaviors. They can really get behind having a job to do. It keeps students busy, focused, and provides a way to gain attention in a more positive, classroom-appropriate way.

When we assign group projects, one thing we can do to encourage that team mindset is to make sure each student in the group has a role to play. One student can be the note taker, another can be the timekeeper, and someone else can be the team captain. Someone can oversee materials. Someone else can make sure the group stays on topic. And these can be made into a really big deal! You can have name tags that have each role written on them. When you do this, you get them to buy in, and you get them motivated to participate. This way everyone is involved, and everyone wins.

Speaking of everyone winning, you can also have the whole class work together to earn a reward. Keep up that team mindset where everyone needs to do their part for the whole class to earn a reward at the end. Having a class reward not only helps each student be accountable, but it also gives students the opportunity to encourage and motivate each other.

My husband is a band director at our local middle school (I know; God bless him). Everything he does, the kids know it will include all of them or none of them, because they are a team. The band can't play with just tubas or just flutes. It takes all of them, working together, toward a common goal. But that isn't particular to only a band class or a sports team. In any classroom, you can try to emulate that by giving students something to strive toward together. It can be something as small as a hard candy or a sticker, free time at the end of class, or even an extra recess.

A few years ago, my class of sixth graders earned a donut party because they collectively completed over 5000 minutes of their Edmentum learning path. One student couldn't have done that on their own. They had to work together to make it happen. And they were so funny when they would talk about it together. I would check how many minutes each student had done for the week and when a student's minutes were lower than they should have been, I didn't have to say a word! The other students took care of it for me with choruses of "What do you mean you didn't do your minutes! Get off that game and do your minutes! I want a donut!" And when the last student completed his last minutes, the cheers could be heard from the front office to the gymnasium. They ran around the room like they just scored the gold medal in the Olympics. They got their donuts, but more important than that, each one of them increased their diagnostic scores. The donuts motivated them, working as a team motivated them, and they were successful in improving their learning.

Finally with collaboration, we are thinking outside of our subject area and thinking about cross-curricular collaboration. So in my classroom, I passed out interest surveys so I could learn a little more about what my students liked, what they might be motivated by, and what they struggled with the most. In one of those input surveys, one of my students, I'll call him Cal, said reading was his least favorite subject. However, he went on to say that Social Studies was his favorite subject. That caught me off guard just a bit because, as we know, Social Studies is a "reading heavy" curriculum.

So what is it then about "reading" that he didn't like? More importantly, how could I utilize the intrinsic motivation he exhibited to somehow encourage and support his journey in reading and ELA? With cross-curricular collaboration. In this case, combining the subject matter that he was interested in with an act and task he enjoyed less. Learning about WWII in Social Studies could lead to a compare and contrast essay in ELA. For Cal, it empowered him and helped him realize that he was a much better reader than he gave himself credit for.

At the middle school I worked in, our Social Studies teacher had the kids do a group presentation on a notable figure, and our ELA teacher helped them develop an annotated bibliography for the report. Taking a subject a student is highly interested in and incorporating it into a subject that has less interest boosts their motivation. It makes them more willing to participate and have a better chance of success.

AUTHENTICITY

When I taught middle school, the students had several phrases they used *all the time*. One of the most used was, "That's cap." If you haven't been around a lot of 12-year-olds recently, let me tell you that "cap" means lying. So when someone was telling a story that was less than believable, the response was "That's cap!" In other words, "I don't believe you." And they were quick to call out someone for being fake or being two-faced. They could see it from a mile away. And that didn't just apply to their peers. If they didn't feel like their teachers were being real with them, they wouldn't be willing to learn from them.

A big part of authenticity in the classroom is building real relationships with our students. I know, I know. You've heard this before. And trust me, I know there's more to running a classroom than "building relationships." However, it really is a key to engaging with students. They need to know we care. They need to know we are a safe space for them and that we are going to keep it real with them. We sometimes feel the same way about our administrators and those higher up. They can have all the extra degrees in the world, but if we teachers don't feel supported and encouraged by our bosses, they won't be effective as leaders.

It's the same for students and teachers. We have to Maslow before we can Bloom. We have to make sure students have basic needs met—feel safe, and like they belong, that they can be themselves—before we can even start to think about academic success. The way we do this is by building authentic relationships with students.

The difference between the common phrase of "building relationships" and being *authentic* in those relationships is all about meeting students where they are and getting to know them as *people* first and academics second. And it needs to be mutual. They need to know you as a person and not just as a teacher. Now, I'm not saying tell your students all your secrets. Obviously, there are some things you should not share with your students. But when it comes to authenticity, students need to know you beyond the role of "teacher," especially if that role has previously come with a negative connotation.

When I was in the classroom, it was important to me that my students knew me as a person. All my students knew the names of my husband, my daughter, and even my pets. They knew my favorite Starbucks order (and sometimes they brought it to me in the mornings).

It's about all the little things that let them get to know you as a person. After all, we teachers aren't robots, and neither are our students. They have feelings just like we do. Our students are often still working on how to process their feelings when difficult situations come up. That means we have the chance to model healthy emotional behavior.

> " The goal of authenticity is to show, through modeling, how healthy people handle big emotions. "

So when you're feeling some kinda way, talk to the kids about it. Model what it should look like to have a big feeling but still maintain self-control. That's real, healthy authenticity.

The goal of authenticity isn't to be too vulnerable or overshare in a way that puts teachers and students at the same level. The goal is to show, through modeling, how healthy people handle big emotions while we are earning our students' trust as "real" people.

I'll give you a personal example. Back in the fall of 2021, I learned that a student I had taught in a multi-disability high school class had passed away due to complications from an illness. This was a young man I had really grown close to. He was so incredibly special to me. As you might imagine, I was heartbroken. The next morning, I got up after a very long night and went to school. I tried not to let my personal sadness affect me in the classroom, but I was struggling. That meant I was being very short with the kids and had much less patience than normal. My students knew that obviously something wasn't right. After a little while, one asked if I was mad at them.

That's when I realized I wasn't being real with them. So I told them I had lost a former student and shared some of the things that made him so special to me. My students were so sweet about it. They showed empathy, and I got a great group hug that made me feel so much better. Trying to hide my emotions from them didn't work. What *did* work was talking to them about it and modeling that it's okay to be sad and have big feelings.

At the same time, it's okay to have fun with your students, too! One fun, easy way to build authentic relationships is by playing "Get to Know You" games. My students loved to play "Would You Rather." I would read a "would you rather" question, and the students and I would run to one side of the room or the other, depending on our answers. They were able to see me engaging with them at their level, and we were able to learn about each other in a fun, low-pressure way.

Another idea is to incorporate a class meeting time. Taking a few moments to just chat about life with your students can make such a difference in the way students view your class and their relationship with you. Take some time dedicated to simply talking together and checking in. This shows them you're willing to listen and you genuinely *care* about what they have to say. When you show an interest in their lives outside of the classroom, it goes far in building those authentic relationships.

Beyond talking and interacting, it's essential that your students know they can trust you. Perhaps the most impactful way to earn their trust is keeping your promises. This might be my number one tip. If you have promised your students something, do everything within your power to keep it. The quickest way to break someone's trust is to break promises, and the kids won't let you forget. They may not remember to bring a pencil to class but they will remember that two weeks ago, you told them they could have ice cream on Friday if they did their work. If it's Friday, they're going to want to know where their ice cream is!

But it can also mean keeping your promise, which I've learned first-hand. I had a 6th grade student, who we'll call Ricardo, who transferred to my school. He entered the classroom very reluctantly. He looked like he had the weight of the world on his shoulders—just mad at everything and everyone. Ricardo didn't trust anybody because everyone he'd trusted had left him. His attitude was one that said, "I'm going to push you away before you have the chance to hurt me."

One particular day, he was engaging in behavior after behavior, and it escalated to cussing out one of his peers. I brought him out in the hallway. He wouldn't make eye contact with me, opting instead to look at the floor, with his hair hanging in his eyes to cover his face. He expected me to yell and for him to get in trouble, because that's what happened in the past. Instead of doing either of those things, I leveled with him. I told him I knew he was angry, and that he had every right to feel that way. I talked to him, person to person rather than teacher to student. I made a promise to him that I would always be straight with him. I wouldn't sugar coat anything. I would tell him exactly why something happened the way it did. And he respected me more for that than for anything else I could have done for him. We went on to have the best relationship. That student who "hated school" and hated teachers told everyone who would listen that I was his favorite.

But the greatest compliment I ever received—not just from him, but from anyone—was when I overheard him talking to another student who was having some issues. He told him, "If you need to talk, you can talk to Mrs. Poe; you can trust her." He didn't know I heard him. He didn't see the tears that sprang to my eyes. He didn't know that him saying that would outweigh any award or accolade I could receive. I still view that as the ultimate testament to being a good teacher—having his trust.

Being authentic and building authentic relationships with your students go so far beyond simply increasing motivation for classroom participation. It can change a student's entire trajectory.

RELEVANCE

Can you remember when you were a student if you ever asked, "When are we ever going to use this in real life?" I know I did, especially when it came to math. I enjoyed math, but I never really expected to need to use the Pythagorean theorem in real life. And I know we still have students like that—who don't see the need to learn what we are trying to teach them because they think it's not relevant. So how can we change that? We must show our students that what we are teaching *does* relate to them, and not only that, but that we relate to them, as well.

One way to build relevance is by using real-world situations and problems in our lessons. In 2021, my 6th grade students were learning about unit rates. Let me rephrase… they were *supposed* to be learning about unit rates, but have you ever tried to teach pubescent 12-year-olds *anything* while their sweat glands and their hormones are fully raging? Because let me tell you, they are not interested.

I'm reminded of a video that circulates around social media. It goes like this:

Principal: *"We need you to teach the children math."*

Teacher: "Do they want to learn math?"
Principal: "No. You have to make them learn it against their will."

Because that's literally what it feels like sometimes. Here we are with a roomful of children who would rather be doing anything else, anywhere else. So we have to make them *want* to be where they are.

I devised a project for the students so that unit rates made a little more sense and were a little more relevant to them. Since we were working on the unit in November, I designed a project where they were given a budget and specifications to develop a Thanksgiving menu and grocery list. They only had $100 to create a menu for six people that included an appetizer, a main dish, three side dishes, a beverage, and a dessert. I included links to several local grocery store ads for them to use. They had to search through the ads and write down the prices of similar items at different stores so they could compare the cost. My students discovered that just because something was "cheaper" on the tag didn't mean it was the lower unit rate. They learned that sometimes it's more affordable to buy the more expensive item instead of having to get two of the lower cost items depending on how much was inside it.

I had a feeling the students would enjoy the activity. I did not anticipate how they would each turn into middle school versions of Ebenezer Scrooge, trying to save every single penny they could. To my surprise, I heard things like, "They want *how much* for a can of corn? What am I? Made of money?" Some even declared that they would oversee planning Thanksgiving that year since they now knew how to do it. Some told me they had already shown their parents their grocery lists to help them save money. Once the students had something relevant to do with the curriculum, they were much more engaged in the lesson.

My general education co-teacher and I spent several days just planning for their success, differentiating the project and accommodating it to meet the needs of our students. We allowed some children to partner up. For others, we helped them make their grocery lists. Some students did not have to find as many menu items as others. However, each student was able to engage with and participate in the project. Those who were not in our co-taught classes even used the project. It wasn't something that was specifically developed for "special education students." It was developed for *all* students. Because that's what inclusion really means.

Another way to keep things relevant is using current events. By tying curriculum into what is happening in the world around them, we can show students why something matters. We can help them relate to the material on a more personal level. And as author Brandon P. Fleming states in his memoir *Miseducated*, "When has anyone ever become passionate about something that wasn't personal" (Fleming, p. 128)?

One of my most favorite lessons used popular song lyrics as examples of literary devices. I could have used classic poems, yes. But my students were much more familiar with Katie Perry and Nicki Manaj than they were with Emily Dickinson or Sylvia Plath. I combined visuals of the singers with their lyrics and the definition of what specific literary device they were using within their songs.

For example, to illustrate a simile, I used Katy Perry and the lyric from "Firework" that says, "Do you ever feel like a plastic bag..." Relating something new, like figurative language, to something already understood, like a popular song, makes the lesson more relatable to them. I encouraged them to find their own examples in songs. Naming the singers made for an excellent prompt for some who needed help remembering which term went with what definition. When we use what they know, students are more likely to want to be involved, which leads to increased participation and engagement, which leads to more learning.

Another way to build relevance in a lesson is to play to a student's interests. At the beginning of each semester, I always liked to give my class interest inventories that I could reference in lessons or when deciding on rewards. In other words, if I decided to reward my students with a donut party, but half of them didn't like donuts, that wouldn't do much to motivate them.

But not every reward or reinforcer needs to be tangible. Some students like public praise or seeing their work posted because it builds up their pride. For some students, that's embarrassing and it would have the exact opposite effect of what I was trying to do. And as the teacher, that's important information to have. We need to know what they do like and what they are interested in so we know how to motivate them.

On the opposite page is the Student Reinforcement Survey I created to learn more about what motivated my students. I would either give this to students to complete independently or I'd go through it with them one at a time so I could make sure they were able to complete it with as much or as little support as necessary.

At one point in my teaching career, I had a student whom I know for a fact I will never forget—for a variety of reasons. I had this kiddo, we'll call him Marcus, about 60% of the day. We were working on several skills that he was missing, both academically and socially/behaviorally. And one of the skills I worked on with him was his ability to complete a task. He would get "bored" and lose interest in an activity within a couple minutes—unless it had to do with Hot Wheels cars. He wanted to play with the cars and build cities and drive them through various cities he created. And while I was able to use that as a reward, I also used it by incorporating cars into our lessons.

One of his goals was to be able to blend CVC words (like cat or dog). Marcus was able to produce the letter sounds individually, but could not blend them together to make a readable word. He would say "/c/ /a/ /t/... BOX!" So using his love of his toy cars, I made him a specially designed blending board.

Student Reinforcement Survey

Complete this inventory by discussing options with your student. Fill in anything specific. Feel free to add ideas from your students.

Student:	
Date Completed:	

Tangible (list favorites)

Candy:	
Salty Snack:	
Sweet Snack:	
Beverage:	
Toy:	
Other:	
Other:	

Attention (circle all that apply)

Display Work in Classroom	Verbal Praise (Public)	Note home
Display Work in Hallway	Verbal Praise (Private)	Phone call home
Time with a preferred friend	Certificate	Time with a preferred staff member (principal, preferred teacher, etc)
Line Leader	Other:	Other:

Activity (circle all that apply)

Puzzles	Dress Up	Computer/Tablet	Blowing bubbles
Play-doh	Sharpening pencils	Time Writing	Board game
Drawing/painting	Books/Reading	Blocks	Listening to music
Other:	Other:	Other:	Other:

It took me approximately one minute using an online design software to make this "Blending Road." He would use his toy car and drive along the road, saying the letter sound as he hit the "potholes" in front of the letters. The faster he drove, the faster he said the letter sounds together. And I watched Marcus do this over and over:

"/c/ /a/ /t/

/c/ /a/ /t/

/c/ /a/ /t/"

Until he stopped. He stopped driving the car and looked up at me with wide eyes and said "CAT! It says CAT!" Marcus erased the letters and exclaimed "Give me another one!" So I wrote another CVC word. He started the process over with his car starting slowly before getting faster and faster. "TOP! It says TOP!"

It was like a secret code had been broken. Letters spelled words—*real words*—that he could read! And the code was broken by incorporating something Marcus loved, something he was willing to stick with and use—a simple Hot Wheels car.

I think of that precious boy every time I see a Hot Wheels car in a store. Each time, I'm reminded that learning what students are interested in makes lessons more relevant and leads to life-changing moments.

Earlier when we were talking about differentiating assessments, one option was doing a presentation or making a video instead of doing a paper/pencil test. My students loved TikTok, which certainly wasn't something we could put down on paper. So I started assigning "TikTok" style videos as assessments. One of my students made a video explaining how to divide fractions. Another group of students wrote lyrics and performed a song all about the multiples of four. It was catchy. We were all singing it for weeks. Other students who struggled with writing were able to explain their knowledge orally and gave some great answers. They showed what they knew in a way that made the most sense to them and in a way they actually enjoyed!

> **Remember, we are grading a child based on what they know—not on how well they can regurgitate information onto a piece of paper.**

The goal of any teacher is not to make a child learn in a certain way, but rather to empower a child to demonstrate their knowledge in the way that makes sense to them. If that's writing a poem, let them write a poem. If it's recording a video, let them record a video. Let them show you what they know. You'll be amazed at what they can come up with and usually you will better be able to see their actual ability and understanding through those methods than through a regular worksheet or test. Remember, we are grading a child based on what they know—not on how well they can regurgitate information onto a piece of paper.

ENGAGEMENT

Student engagement is another one of those educational buzzwords, and it kind of encapsulates everything else we've been discussing. As educators, it is our duty to ensure our students are active, engaged participants in their own education. Brandon P. Fleming writes about learning to meet his students where they were in order to increase engagement within them:

> "I soon learned that there is a difference between being uninterested and being disengaged. We often accuse young people of being uninterested in matters we consider important, but seldom do adults claim responsibility for our failure to engage with them at their level" (p. 158).

Increasing student engagement increases their participation which in turn increases overall achievement. So how do we make sure our students are staying consistently engaged?

The first way is variety. It's been proven that we remember something more when it's unexpected. For instance, if an elephant walked by your front door while you were reading this book, you might remember some of what you were reading, but you'd definitely remember that there was an elephant, because it was unexpected. Likewise, if you're constantly doing the same types of lessons, they're all going to run together. They're not going to be memorable. So let's throw in some variety. This would be a great time for a room transformation if you're the type of teacher who wants to try that out. And you can make it as big or as simple as you want.

In my teaching career, I decorated and "transformed" classrooms quite a few times. Once, I set up my daughter's galaxy projector (that I borrowed from my house) and played songs from Star Wars while students participated in Star Wars themed math activities. It was different; it was exciting. They were eager to participate because it was something outside our classroom norm. Another time, I decorated the classroom to look like a pizzeria and used pizza-themed centers to work on ELA activities. Again, changing it up from our usual pace had them so engaged, even in centers they completed independently.

Now a caveat to that—even with the variety in the lessons and the fun decorations, the classroom expectations *did not change*. Our routines stayed consistent, and our procedures stayed the same. There is a difference in adding variety into your lessons and changing classroom expectations. For most if not all students, they need those explicitly taught and consistent routines and procedures so they know what behavior is expected. You can add variety to your lessons, but keep the expectations, routines, and procedures the same so students are able to maintain consistency.

Some teachers are not classroom transformation teachers, and that is completely fine! If your students cannot handle change or if you are still working with them about meeting classroom expectations when the room is the same as it always is, do not do it. If you personally don't want to, don't do it. There are other ways to increase engagement with variety such as offering choice.

My last year teaching sixth grade, I had a student, I'll call him Eric. Getting him to write his answers or take notes on paper was a daily struggle. Eric would start writing, and then stop. He'd copy every other math problem. He'd finish writing half a sentence and tell me his hand hurt and he couldn't write any more. It was a constant battle of telling him to pick up his pencil and get back to work.

One day, as we were completing assignments in our math notebooks, and my little guy was beyond unengaged, I told him he could pick two of my very special flair pens to complete his work. His eyes lit up. He walked with purpose to my desk and scanned the colorful pens in the little ceramic container. He carefully selected red and black and walked back to his seat. And he completed every single math problem in his notebook.

We continued this routine of him selecting his pens every day at the beginning of class, and soon his notebook was filled with colorful answers. Did you read that right? Let me rephrase that sentence: his notebook was filled with *answers*. It didn't matter what color they were or that they were written with pen instead of pencil. He was able to show me what he knew, and he did so willingly. Just by changing it up a little bit and adding in some variety, we went from a daily battle to a student who was engaged and participatory.

A second way to increase student engagement is to utilize brain breaks throughout the day. Brain breaks are just small pauses in a lesson to allow for extra movement. They can be talking to a friend or finding a change of scenery. Whatever you choose, know that brain breaks can help you regain student engagement after the break is completed.

You know what your students look like when they're losing interest. They look out the window. They play with their pencils. They sneak their phones out of their pockets or open new tabs on their devices. Those moments are the perfect time for a brain break, a simple reset to change up what's happening and bring them back to focus.

Think about when you're in a faculty meeting or training session and the speaker goes on and on and your eyes start glazing over and you start thinking about what you are going to make for dinner or perhaps that load of laundry that's still sitting in the washer. When that happens, you aren't engaged. I'm the same way. But if the speaker offers a short break, and I can use the restroom or get water (or more likely another cup of coffee), I'm ready to get back into it. If we as adults need breaks, kids need them even more. They don't need to be very long—just something so they can get up, get a break, get some wiggles out, and be ready to come back and focus.

There are different types of brain breaks you can use depending on what you are trying to accomplish and what your students need. Pay attention to what they look like when they need a brain break. Are they falling asleep? Do they need to boost their energy? Let's have a 30 second dance party to get everyone up out of their seats and get some blood pumping! On the other hand, are they a little too wild and they need some mental focus? Turn on some mindful breathing exercises and help them calm their bodies and minds. Let their behavior dictate what kind of break you give them. Consider limiting it to just a few minutes, and then get back into the lesson or transition to the next activity.

Establishing a positive and supportive classroom culture doesn't have to be a daunting task. Finding what your students enjoy, being real with them, and engaging with them on their level all work together to help you build those relationships. Small changes to your classroom routine and lessons can have a big impact when it comes to making your classroom an inclusive environment where students *want* to be and feel like they truly belong.

CHAPTER 6:
COLLABORATIVE TEAMWORK

In my teaching career, I had the opportunity to work with all types of educators—some were older or younger, some had different cultures and heritages. Each brought a new and different point of view to the table. It was exciting to be a part of such eclectic teams, but it could be overwhelming, also, as I wondered how we would be able to come together as a group to support our students. Some of these teachers became my close friends: we texted and hung out on the weekends, we shared lesson plans, we brought each other coffee, and we hung out together during planning periods.

> " When teachers, staff, and families work together, we create an inclusive, equitable, and empowering educational environment for all students. "

However there were other teachers I worked with where a close relationship didn't happen. Our personalities were too different; we had varying ideas of what to do in the classroom and opposing views on how to work with the students. Even though we weren't as good of "friends" as I was with others, it was still vital that we presented a unified front and communicated with respect and empathy toward one another.

As my mama used to tell me, "You don't have to get along with everyone, but you still need to show respect." I'm not telling you that you must be best friends with everyone you work with. What I am telling you is that you must maintain a professional working relationship with each of them.

In the journey towards inclusive education, there is a critical step teachers must take. We need to forge strong and effective partnerships between general education teachers, special education teachers, support staff, and families. These connections are the key to success in the world of special education. These partnerships are not merely beneficial, but rather indispensable. Working together with both general education and special education personnel makes our schools more inclusive and promotes a greater chance of success for every student. When teachers, staff, and families work together, we create an inclusive, equitable, and empowering educational environment for all students.

BUILDING EFFECTIVE PARTNERSHIPS WITH TEACHERS AND FAMILIES

So often, we hear that the first thing we need to do when we get a new group of students is build relationships with them. However, that is just as true for every member of the special education team. When we talked about IEPs, we discussed the fact that IEPs are developed and agreed upon by an entire team: the IEP team, consisting of the special education teacher, the general education teacher, the family, and any related service providers in addition to a lead education agency representative (often a principal). It is essential that we build effective partnerships where each member feels valued, seen, and heard.

So how do we do that? How do we make sure that we are creating a team?

COMMUNICATING WITH OTHER TEACHERS

Working closely together as a team is one of the best ways to ensure inclusive instruction and make sure each student is receiving exactly what they need to be as successful as possible.

When you do this with your co-teacher or team, you will each be able to share what works for what student and vice versa. You will be able to tag in and out and bounce off one another and the potential is there to create true magic in the classroom. But I know during the school day, you are BUSY. How are you supposed to share all this knowledge and plan together when you have a roomful of 30+ students and only so many hours in the day?

One thing I recommend is to create a running Google Doc that is shared between you and your student's general education teacher. Choose different colors of font so it is easy to differentiate who wrote what, and as you remember something, type it in the doc so it's shared right away. That's always easier than trying to remember something to say an hour later or writing it on a sticky note that can easily disappear. You can organize your doc by class or even by student if there is a particular individual who requires a lot of extra support or attention.

Another option is with a Google form. I personally loved this option when I needed to collect behavior data on a student. On the form, there was a space for the student's name, class period, date, and time. There was a space for a quick note about the student's behavior and a rating scale (1-5) about the severity of the student's behavior with a very clear rubric about what each number meant. I made QR codes that my co-teachers could scan with their phones that would take them right to the form for each particular student.

Google forms and docs were so easy to set up and quick to use. That way each person was able to contribute and conversations can flow—even with limited time to speak in person. Doing so allowed each person on the team to be able to contribute. I no longer had to run from room to room with charts and clipboards attempting to collect data from a teacher who was also trying to teach 30 other students in the classroom at the same time.

COMMUNICATING WITH FAMILIES: KEEP THE CONVERSATION GOING

Google forms were another great way to get family input in an efficient way. I always loved that it didn't result in making copy after copy to send home again and again. If I needed input for a student's IEP or if a general education teacher wanted to submit a pre-conference questionnaire, it was always so much simpler to email out a google link. Not only did it give the family immediate access to the form, but it also provided digital storage for the results that I could print to put in the student's file. Usually, families appreciated not having one more piece of paper to keep up with, and as a mom myself, I could totally relate!

Another crucial aspect of communicating with families is finding a way to have conversations and relay information quickly without giving families your personal phone number. I remember when I learned that lesson.

My first year teaching, I gave my phone number out as a way for parents and guardians to get in touch with me because I did not have a phone in my classroom, and I wasn't able to leave class to answer a phone call in the office. As a young teacher, I wanted families to be able to contact me as needed so that they always felt included and up-to-date with the goings on of their children. Most families did not take advantage.

However, there were some who would text me late at night or on weekends. They got mad when I didn't respond in what they considered a "timely manner." I tried explaining that I was not available after hours (and especially on weekends), and that their messages would be returned the next school day. But I was awful at setting boundaries. I felt guilty, so sometimes I ended up in a conversation on my own time, which took away from time I could have been spending with my family. The next school year, I changed tactics and only emailed or called from a school phone.

If you want to give out your number, you do you. But if not, there are several different applications you can use to communicate with families that do not involve giving it out. In previous schools where I've worked, we've used ClassDojo. It allows families and teachers to exchange private messages, teachers to share class announcements, and photo sharing. It also has "quiet hours" teachers can set up that lets families know that their message has been sent outside of the teacher's responding hours. It's a great way to keep families in the loop without crossing any boundaries.

POSITIVE COMMUNICATION FOR POSITIVE RELATIONSHIPS

So we've talked about ways to communicate with families. Now we'll shift gears and discuss *how* we should be communicating with families. Simply talking to one another does not guarantee a strong relationship. It's all about *how* you talk to one another, or more importantly, how *you* talk to the family.

Often, students receiving special education services are going to have a hard time either academically or behaviorally. We know it. Their families know it too. They don't need to be constantly reminded of their child's struggles. When communicating with families, it is important to take a "strengths-based" approach at the beginning of building your relationship. Talk about what their student did well. Discuss how their student was able to improve in one area.

The first time you contact a family should not be to tell them their child got in trouble. If you are a parent, imagine how that would make you feel? If you aren't, imagine your principal spoke to your parent or partner for the first time and the first thing they did was complain about you. Personally, that would make me feel bad and probably make me very defensive and hesitant to form a partnership with that person. That's how our students' families feel when the first thing they hear from us is something negative about their child.

Starting from a strengths-based approach and sharing something positive about their student helps a relationship to form. It shows the family that you enjoy their child and want them to succeed. It shows that you celebrate their child with them. Then later, if something happens and you need to get in touch with a family for a negative reason, you've already laid that foundation of mutual respect. That means they'll be much more likely to listen when you tell them something is wrong. It also helps you both be more likely to look for a positive solution as a team.

As a newly hired second grade teacher in 2022, I wanted to reach out to the families of my new students who would be experiencing a new special education case manager for the first time in their school careers. I called families and spoke to some. I left voicemails for others. One call was returned by the mother of a student I will call Travis. When I called his mom, she immediately began making excuses—Travis had a hard year last year. He gets frustrated because he can't read as well as his peers. Travis is a good kid if I "give him a chance."

Amid these statements, I interrupted her. "Ma'am," I said since I'm from the south. "Travis is precious. I can tell he's already trying hard. He's enjoying helping hand out small group supplies, and his quick wit keeps me laughing. I think we're going to have a great year."

Travis's mom thanked me for getting in touch with her, and we hung up the phone. I made a mental note to continue to reach out to her. Whether it was a quick email or sending home a small note or some classwork with Travis, I wanted her to know, I was looking for the good—something all students deserve.

Eventually, I did have to get in touch with Travis's mom, because although her son and I had a good relationship, there were some things happening in and out of my classroom that required her support. She was so receptive to that phone call. And she was ready and willing to support me as I supported him. Because not only did Travis and I have a good relationship, his mother and I had one, too. She knew I cared for her son. She also knew he was capable, so when behaviors crept up that were outside of the norm, we sought a solution as a team. Had I waited to contact her until there was a problem, I know that conversation would have not ended well. She would have seen me as someone opposite from her and her child instead of one who was on their team. Positive interaction *matters* for all students.

I want you to do something for me. We are going to do an exercise I like to call "Making a List" (I know; it's super creative). But just go with it. You'll need something to write with and something to write on.

Now, without looking, think about your class roster. Set a timer for 90 seconds and write your students' names on your sheet of paper before the time runs out.

Now look at the list of names, and ask yourself some questions:

1. Whose names did you write down first? Are they students you most call out during class? Are they the ones who answer all the questions? Why do they have so much of your attention?

2. Whose names fell in the middle? What characteristics come to mind when you think of these students?

3. Whose names came to your mind last? What can you do to build a better connection with those students?

This list can be revealing. For some, the students you might have thought of first are the ones who you are constantly calling out for misbehaving. Or perhaps they're the "good" kids who you know will always have their hands raised. What about the students at the end of your list? Are they just getting by in your classroom? Are they not causing behavior problems, but also not really participating in the learning environment?

The next time you're in the classroom, try to look for something positive about each student in your classroom, especially for the students you don't think about as often or as positively as the others. Plan to contact the students' families (either a phone call, email, or note home) to share that positive thing you thought of for each of their students. Share that positive thing with the students' too. Lay the foundation for positive communication and work purposely on improving relationships.

TROUBLESHOOTING COMMUNICATION PROBLEMS

"Okay," I hear you say. "That's all well and good, but what happens when the family doesn't reciprocate?"

I've been there. I've had students whose families I literally never laid eyes on. I've had messages left on "read" and voicemails that were never returned. With some families, it felt like no matter what I did, I couldn't get a response. But I kept trying. I kept calling, emailing, and sending notes home. And I documented everything. Because one thing I would not allow to happen was for a family to say I never got in touch with them. Because I had the receipts! A common phrase in special education is "If it's not documented, did it really happen?" And that applies to efforts to contact families.

So, make sure you keep a call log. Save those outbound emails, and document, document, document!

But what about the families who don't return your positive professional attitude with one of their own? Because that also happens. I'll say to you what I say to my students: You cannot control someone else's actions; you can only control your own. People are going to respond the way they are going to respond. My advice to you is not to add fuel to their fire. Of course, I know that is easier said than done. It is our human nature to respond to anger with anger. But that will not do a thing to improve the situation, and can possibly harm you in the end, so do your very best to not take angry parents personally. Return their anger with professionalism and be the bigger person.

However, please rest assured that I am not telling you to tolerate malice, threats, or public disrespect. If that's the case, speak with your principal and let them know what's going on. You do not have to deal with that kind of parent on your own, nor should you.

CO-TEACHING: ROLES AND DESIGN

There is another type of partnership that goes beyond co-*workers*, and that is the relationship between co-*teachers*. With a co-teaching design, a general education teacher and a special education teacher are assigned to the same class. If that's the case for you, then a successful co-teaching relationship is essential for your students to be able to get everything out of the learning environment possible in the way that makes the most sense for them. But it doesn't happen without effort from both teachers. Open communication about different types of co-teaching styles and what types of roles each person will play is required to avoid misunderstandings, hurt feelings, and discord in the classroom.

CO-TEACHING MODELS

Just like there is no "one-size-fits-all" method when it comes to teaching our students, there is no "one-size-fits-all" method when it comes to co-teaching, either. You and your partner will have to determine what model works best for you—and that might change depending on the subject or the needs of your students during different class periods. It might even change based on the specific activities you are doing each day. There is no model that is necessarily better than any other, and each serves a purpose. So let's look at the pros and cons, along with when you might need to use a certain model.

One Teach, One Observe
<u>What is it?</u> In the "One Teach, One Observe" model of co-teaching, one teacher is leading a lesson while another teacher is monitoring the classroom, collecting observation data regarding a student or group of students.
<u>What are the pros?</u> • One teacher can collect data in real time for IEPs, 504s, FBAs, etc.
<u>What are the cons?</u> • If one teacher is always leading the lesson and the other is always observing, students might view one teacher as having more authority than the other • It's not a true model of "co-teaching" as only one teacher is doing the teaching in the classroom
<u>When would you use this model?</u> You might consider using this strategy when behavior data is due for a student or when a teacher needs to collect an observation for evaluation purposes. This model should only be used as necessary to collect data or conduct observations and should not be the standard model used day-to-day.

One Teach, One Assist

<u>What is it?</u>

In the "One Teach, One Assist" model, one teacher is leading a lesson while another is walking throughout the classroom providing support to those students who need a bit of extra help.

<u>What are the pros?</u>

- One teacher is available to provide real-time support to students as needed
- Students can receive help without interrupting the lesson for everyone else
- One teacher can curb problematic behaviors without the lesson having to pause

<u>What are the cons?</u>

- If one teacher is always leading the lesson and the other is always providing support, students might view them as having more authority than their partner.
- If used improperly, it may create "learned helplessness" for students who always receive 1:1 support

<u>When would you use this model?</u>

You might consider using this strategy when one teacher is more familiar with the subject matter or teaching strategy than another, or when you know there will be students who have greater need for 1:1 support (behaviorally or academically) during the lesson.

Station Teaching

What is it?

In the "Station Teaching" model of co-teaching, students are divided into multiple groups (3 or more). Academic "stations" are set up around the room with at least one independent station while the two teachers lead two other stations. Students will alternate stations, each working with both teachers and the independent station until everyone has completed the rotation.

What are the pros?

- Both teachers are actively teaching in the classroom
- Teachers can utilize multiple modalities to teach the same concept in different ways
- It keeps lessons short—maintaining student focus by "resetting" when groups rotate
- It lowers the student to teacher ratio, allowing students to receive more direct instruction and helps maintain order in the classroom

What are the cons?

- It requires extensive preparation to ensure students know how to utilize the stations
- Students at the independent station might cause a distraction for the others
- Students at the independent station might have questions and interrupt a teaching station
- Students and teachers might not work at the same pace, so rotations might end at different times or students might not make it through an entire lesson

When would you use this model?

You might consider using this strategy when students need differentiated instruction or accommodations. You might also use it if a classroom has a larger number of students.

Parallel Teaching

<u>What is it?</u>

In the "Parallel Teaching" model of co-teaching, students are divided into two groups—half with one teacher and half with the other. Both cover the same material at the same time. Students will not rotate.

<u>What are the pros?</u>

- Both teachers are actively teaching in the classroom
- Teachers can utilize multiple modalities to teach the same concept in different ways
- You can separate students who do not work well together
- It lowers the student to teacher ratio, allowing students to receive more direct instruction and helps maintain order in the classroom

<u>What are the cons?</u>

- It requires pre-planning to make sure both teachers are covering the same material
- Lessons might not start or end at the same time, so some material might not be covered in one group
- It is essentially two classes occurring at the same time in the same classroom; it might get loud or be distracting to students or teachers

<u>When would you use this model?</u>

You might consider using this strategy if both teachers know the content area very well or if the class is large and splitting it in half might provide a solution.

Alternative Teaching

What is it?

In the "Alternative Teaching" model of co-teaching, students are divided into two groups with one group being smaller than the other.

What are the pros?

- Both teachers are actively teaching in the classroom
- It lowers the student to teacher ratio, allowing students to receive more direct instruction and helps maintain order in the classroom
- It allows students to receive extra support without feeling "singled out"
- It allows opportunities for groups to receive additional support or additional challenges based on need

What are the cons?

- Teachers must analyze data before grouping students
- Students in the small group might miss out on instruction happening in the large group
- It can lead to stigmatization of students who are "always in the small group"

When would you use this model?

You might consider using this strategy if there is a core group of students who regularly need more support or more of a challenge or if there is a need for pre—or re-teaching.

Team Teaching

<u>What is it?</u>

In the "Team Teaching" model of co-teaching, both teachers are actively teaching the whole group and walking around providing extra support to students who need it.

<u>What are the pros?</u>

- Both teachers are actively teaching in the classroom
- It gives two sets of eyes to actively monitor students for classroom management and for academic support
- It doubles up on the level of knowledge and skills a teacher brings to a classroom
- It models collaboration and teamwork

<u>What are the cons?</u>

- Teachers must have planning time together to review resources, prepare and plan material, and give grades
- Teachers must be able to have a professional relationship and not exhibit disrespect toward each other, especially when in front of students

---

<u>When would you use this model?</u>

You might consider using this strategy to increase instructional models and modalities for students who need it.

CO-TEACHING STRATEGIES

No matter the co-teaching model you follow, there are some strategies you will have to implement to make sure you are making the most of your co-teaching class time.

1. **Assigning Roles**

    When working with a co-teacher, it is essential that you both understand and accept the roles you are going to play in the classroom. If one teacher is going to lead the lesson and one is going to provide support to smaller groups or individual students, that needs to be established before class begins. Both teachers' opinions should be considered when deciding who is going to do what.

2. **Understanding Student Needs**

   If you are co-teaching students with IEPs along with a special education teacher, it is just as much your responsibility to be familiar with the students' IEPs (including goals, services, accommodations, and related services) as it is for the special education teacher. Both teachers will create and provide accommodations, differentiate instruction, and abide by the IEP. Take some time at the beginning of the year to make sure you understand the students' IEPs with the special education teacher so you can both be sure you are providing each student what they need to be successful.

3. **Ensuring Mutual Expectations**

   One classroom with two teachers can be difficult for students to navigate if each has a different set of expectations for students to follow. Decide at the beginning what your routines and procedures will be. Decide what will be allowed or not allowed so students aren't confused on what is expected. And when expectations are not met, make sure that both of you are following through with consequences equally to avoid power struggles. If the rule is no gum in class, and one of you is more lenient than the other, students may begin seeing one teacher as the "good guy" and the other as the "bad guy." Being on the same page avoids that. The same can be said for giving grades. Having a rubric can help when it comes to grading so you know what you are looking for in an assignment. You want to be a unified front when teaching your class together.

   > **A positive co-teaching experience doesn't happen by accident. It takes intention and determination.**

4. **Collaborating for Positive Outcomes**

   Take the time to get to know one another. Not only will this help you get a feel for the other's personal teaching style, but you will also be able to preempt many of the potential issues that can arise due to teaching differences. Building a bond of mutual respect will help stop the previously mentioned "power struggles" from happening in the first place. When you collaborate, you'll need to work together to plan lessons, activities, and assessments. You will also need to have time to meet after a lesson to go over how it went, if any material wasn't covered, or if anything needs to be added or removed for next time.

Co-teaching can be one of the best ways to provide inclusive education and meet all the needs of your class. However, a positive co-teaching experience doesn't happen by accident. It takes intention and determination to overcome differences and decide that you are both going to do what it takes to provide your students with the greatest opportunity for success.

CHAPTER 7:
DIFFERENTIATING INSTRUCTION

When discussing inclusive education, there are three pillars that build a solid foundation for students to be able to access the general education curriculum in the way that works best for them. Differentiation, accommodations, and modifications provide the framework that allows every student not only to acquire new information and skills, but also to actively engage in a variety of aspects of the curriculum that could otherwise be out of reach.

Differentiation, which deals with altering classroom instruction, helps provide alternative methods for students to learn material. Accommodations level the playing field, so to speak, in giving students with disabilities the tools they need to participate. Modifications take it a step further and alter the content making it more attainable based on a student's level of need or ability. Each of these practices make it so that classrooms and teachers can meet the needs of all their students.

In my years of teaching, I can see a clear difference between the years I didn't fully understand these concepts and the years I did. As you might imagine, my classrooms, and students, were more successful once they were utilized. Let's take a closer look at each.

DIFFERENTIATING INSTRUCTION

Within education, the term "differentiation" refers to adapting instruction to meet the needs of a classroom full of diverse learners, with and without disabilities. Every student in your classroom is unique—with different interests, skills, and challenges. A "one-size-fits-all" approach to learning will not cut it. Differentiation is not a single skill or strategy, but rather an approach to education that implements a variety of evidence-based strategies across all areas of the classroom environment: from where you are teaching and what you are teaching (which is the environment and content) to how you are teaching and the outcome of your teaching (the process and product).

DIFFERENTIATION IN THE ENVIRONMENT

The physical classroom space often makes a first impression on your students even before you get a chance to talk and interact with them. What does your classroom say about you and your beliefs about inclusive education? Classroom decorations and materials are a great way to show that your classroom is for *all* students: all cultures, religions, races, abilities...everyone.

> **When it comes to your classroom, all students should be represented.**

But the space shouldn't just be representative of all your students; it should also be accessible for everyone. Consider spacing between furniture or rugs for students who use wheelchairs. Be mindful of students with sensory needs so the classroom isn't overstimulating. And make sure your routines and classroom expectations meet the different needs of your students, as well.

When it comes to your classroom, all students should be represented. They should be able to see themselves in posters and materials and books. They should be able to see students who are different from them represented, also. This shows and teaches students that differences should be celebrated and that everyone can learn from each other.

My beautiful friend, Dr. Deonna Smith, talks about this need:

> "Students need to feel safe before they can be academically successful. A critical element of safety is feeling seen and celebrated for who you are. When students don't see themselves in the learning and in the community space they aren't able to fully engage in the learning. For many students of minority groups, the classroom is a window, a place that they can see other experiences from the outside. They can peer in and learn about others, but are not integrated into the space. What we need is more mirrors, spaces where these students can see the beauty of their own experiences reflected back to them" (Smith, 2023).

In addition to representing your students, your classroom environment should also be accessible for everyone. This means physically accessible, but also designed in such a way that it is learner focused. Instagram and Pinterest can play a large role in influencing the design of classrooms, but who are those designs for? Are they fun for the teacher? Or are they usable for the students?

At the time I am writing this book, Taylor Swift's ERAS tour is in full swing. Everything is pink and sparkly and mirror-balled and stinking adorable. And those vibes are carrying over into classroom decor across the nation! Fun swirly fonts are used on the cutest labels. Colors are mixed and matched, and there is glitter on anything that will stay still long enough to be "bejeweled." Likewise, Instagram and Pinterest are *filled* with perfectly staged images of things aesthetic dreams are made of. But at what cost?

Please hear me and understand me when I say this: There is nothing wrong with having a cute classroom. There is nothing wrong with making your classroom Pinterest-worthy and filling your camera roll with aesthetic pictures of your adorable classroom decor. But when you are planning your classroom theme and decorations, accessibility should be the first consideration you make when deciding if you're going to use something or choose something else: in everything from floor plans to fonts.

In the summer of 2024, I shared this graphic on my Instagram account.

Most of my audience understood what I was implying. Are the fonts cute? Absolutely. Are they accessible? Not so much. For students with dysgraphia or students who are learning the English language or students who are learning to read in general, these fonts do not support their needs in the classroom. Instead, you should opt for fonts that utilize standard letter formations and appropriate capitalization. You can still make it cute, but more importantly, you should make it functional.

If you are having a hard time reading all of these fonts, imagine if you had a reading disability and this was your classroom.

(Just something to think about as you go back to school.)

REBEKAH PO

Another consideration to make when planning for your classroom layout and design is an area students can utilize when they need to take a break or calm down. This area should be separate from the whole group, but still within eyesight for the teacher. Blankets, pillows, and sensory tools like fidgets, lava lamps, or a stuffed animal can provide sensory stimulation for students who need to regulate their emotions in a safe space. You might also consider adding a "think sheet" or blank paper for students to write or draw about how they are feeling.

Teachers should also be mindful of colors, posters, and lights used in the classroom. Choose a limited pallet of calming colors or neutrals with a couple pops of color. When it comes to the walls, less is more—not every surface of your classroom needs to be covered. Anchor charts are great, but try alternating the ones you keep out based on the standards you are currently covering to avoid too much visual clutter. And speaking of visuals, try to utilize natural light from windows. Think about using lamps or string lights (if possible) instead of fluorescent lighting. Or if you must use fluorescent lighting, consider covering some of them with a filter to lessen the harshness.

On the floor, keep desks, tables, and shelves spread apart enough that students (and teachers) can comfortably navigate between them. Try to keep backpacks, bags, and jackets hanging on the backs of chairs or on hooks to keep the floor free of clutter. Low-pile rugs are better for wheelchair users than "shag" rugs. And make sure the exits are not blocked in case of emergency.

Differentiation in the Environment
Fonts: • Each character is a simple, familiar shape   • Each character looks distinct from one another   • Characters have enough spacing between them   • Limit font variations   • Utilize capital letters appropriately   • Use appropriate sizing and a higher contrast
Accessible Fonts to Consider: • Calibri   • Century Gothic   • Futura   • Helvetica   • KG Blank Space   • KG Red Hands   • Poppins   • Tahoma   • Verdana

Walls:

- Leave space to display student work
- Choose specific visuals (posters or anchor charts) that align with the current standard being taught rather than displaying too many visuals

Floor:

- Leave space to navigate between tables, desks, and shelves
- Consider a low-pile rug for students who use wheelchairs or have other mobility concerns
- Keep backpacks, bags, and jackets off the floor to keep walkways clear
- Create separate areas of the classroom using dividers to avoid too much open space for running around

Colors:

- Consider a limited pallet of calming colors
- Keep bold colors to a minimum
- In designs, ensure colors have enough contrast to be clearly visible

DIFFERENTIATION IN THE CONTENT

Another area where teachers can focus on differentiation is the content of their instruction. In this setting, "content" refers to what the teacher expects the students to learn. Differentiating content occurs when students are taught the same skill or concept, but the way in which it's taught can vary depending on student need and ability. There are several strategies that can be incorporated when it comes to differentiating content including tiered and/or scaffolded content, a variety of presentation styles, and varying materials.

Tiering content allows teachers to group students based on readiness and provide content that matches the students' levels. The complexity level can be increased or decreased depending on if students are more advanced and need an extra challenge, or if they require additional support. For example, if students are being taught to write an informative essay, some who are up for a greater challenge might be able to independently research their topic and find outside sources. However, students who require additional support might be working on creating a topic sentence with supporting details.

Not only does the level of complexity vary, but the way the content is presented should vary, as well. When introducing a new concept, the best practice is to give students multiple ways to access the material.

Let's pretend I am getting ready to teach about the water cycle. In order for my students to get a better grasp of this new concept, I will present the information to them in a variety of ways:

- YouTube video: I might start the lesson by playing a video that introduces and explains the water cycle. I will make sure that the video I have chosen is age-appropriate for my students so that the terms used and explanations given do not go over their heads.

- Graphic Organizer: During the video or during group instruction, I might have the students complete a graphic organizer for their notes: to cover the vocabulary terms used and to label the parts of the water cycle

- Experiment: To make the content even more concrete, we might conduct an experiment in which we create condensation and observe what happens.

Each of these ideas demonstrate the same concept, but by differentiating the way it is presented, I will allow my students the opportunity to learn the concept in the way that works best for them. For students who are struggling readers, using a video allows them to access the information in a spoken form so they can hear it and comprehend it better than trying to read it for themselves. Conducting an experiment makes the concept more concrete so they can experience the water cycle instead of just hearing or reading about it. The graphic organizer helps students make sense of the important terms and be able to go back and study them as needed.

Additionally, students can use a variety of learning materials. Going back to the section regarding the informative essay, content can be differentiated by allowing students to choose their own topics. They are much more likely to remain engaged with a lesson for two reasons: if they can clearly see how it is relevant to them and if they are interested in it. Allowing students to choose their own topics automatically boosts student engagement and participation because they can choose something they enjoy or want to learn more about.

In their article "The Five Dimensions of Differentiation," authors Reis and Renzulli state, "In reading, for example, advanced self-selected reading materials would be used to challenge talented readers and less than challenging but high interest content would be used to engage struggling readers."

> **By differentiating the way it is presented, I will allow my students the opportunity to learn the concept in the way that works best for them.**

While some content differentiation can be done in smaller groups and rotations, it is possible to differentiate whole group instruction, too. Take the example lesson I gave about the water cycle, for instance. All of that can be done in a whole group. For the informative essay, a rubric for grading can be used for each essay regardless of topic chosen or reading material used. In other words, you do not have to create multiple lesson plans to differentiate content.

Another way to differentiate content is called scaffolding— a process in which a teacher incorporates supports to enhance students' learning and help them master tasks. In scaffolding, the teacher uses the students' experiences or pre-existing knowledge of a subject or standard to build more competency around that topic. This can be done in three steps: Pre-teaching, during teaching, and post-teaching.

In pre-teaching, teachers explore what students already know, introduce important terms, and allow the class to make predictions about what they think might happen. This is when the "I Do, We Do, You Do" portion of instruction might take place. This is where the teacher first models a task, then the teacher and students complete the task together, and finally, students attempt the task independently in post-teaching. After the lesson, students can summarize it, writing a retelling of it or retelling it to a partner or to a group. This will let you know if your students are ready to move on or if they need another pass at it.

Varying materials and presentation styles in addition to tiering or scaffolding instruction helps each student get and use what they need to access the curriculum content in the way that makes the most sense for them. It is not something that requires multiple lesson plans but instead utilizes multiple approaches. Differentiating content allows teachers to play to their students' strengths and interests in the classroom. This leads to greater engagement and an increased level of learning.

Differentiation in the Content
Tiered Content: • Student groups based on ability level • Increased or decreased level of complexity
Presentation Style: • Visual: video, images, watching a task being modeled • Auditory: recording, class discussion, read aloud • Kinesthetic: experiments, creating a model, acting/roleplaying

Varying Materials: • Student Choice: allow students to choose material based on interest   • Student Need: give students materials that are at their individual instructional levels
Scaffolding Instruction: • Pre-teaching   • Post-teaching   • "I do, We do, You do"

DIFFERENTIATION IN THE INSTRUCTIONAL PROCESS

After content is given, it is time for students to put their newly learned skills to use through the instructional process. When we talk about "process" in this context, we mean the learning experiences crafted to help students interpret, comprehend, and apply the content. The process is the time when students can really dive into a new concept or skill and wrap their brains around it. Just like we differentiated the content, we can also differentiate the process.

A simple way to differentiate "process" is with learning centers or stations. I always loved conducting learning stations in my classroom. It helped me make smaller groups of students so I could work with one group while other groups completed independent activities. Utilizing learning stations allowed me to incorporate a variety of instructional materials to help a concept make more sense for my students while engaging them based on their interests. I could even go a step further and differentiate each station based on ability and readiness level. This does take a bit of work initially to set up stations and teach students how to go through them, but it can make a big difference in your instruction.

When it comes to differentiating the process, you might have some learners who are more capable of researching a topic on their own. With those students, facilitating instruction rather than leading instruction allows them the chance to delve deeper into a topic and learn about it independently. Others may require more direct, explicit instruction—as is often the case with students with disabilities. By providing both pathways, everyone can learn in the way that is best for them.

Another easy way to provide differentiation is to give students materials that make learning more "hands-on." These manipulatives are tangible objects that students can use to build a conceptual understanding of a topic or skill. Utilizing manipulatives helps teachers demonstrate abstract concepts in a more concrete way. For example, cutting a pizza into eight slices is a fun way to demonstrate the concept of fractions. Letting students use blocks or counters to represent numbers helps increase 1:1 correspondence rather than simply rote counting.

Many of my former second grade students really struggled understanding the concept of "regrouping" when it came to subtraction. Where did the ten go? Where did the ones come from? Why can't we just subtract the *other* way? Manipulatives were the solution to this.

I used base ten blocks to represent the tens and the ones. Students "built" out two-digit numbers with the "lines" representing the tens and the small cubes representing the ones. When we needed to regroup to subtract the ones, the students were able to take one of their tens and exchange it for ten indi-

vidual cubes. We lined up the ten individual cubes right next to the line of ten to show how they were the same. They could then see how they had one less ten, but it really wasn't gone; it was just exchanged for ten ones so we could subtract.

A few of my students were able to understand this concept through drawing, and one was able to understand it mentally. However, for those who needed it, the manipulatives helped them *literally* grasp the concept of regrouping with their own hands.

Differentiation in the process helps students grasp concepts in the way that makes the most sense for them. Some might need extended time and manipulatives to really be able to make an abstract concept come to life in a way that they can truly understand. Other students might be able to work a little more independently to understand a concept. By utilizing various strategies and materials, teachers can make sure each student is given the chance to explore a new concept and understand it well enough to problem-solve various solutions.

Differentiation in the Process

Learning Centers:

- Small Group Instruction
- Opportunity for independent practice
- Designed by ability

Manipulatives:

- Make abstract concepts more concrete
- Represent and demonstrate understanding of a concept in a "hands on" way

Extended Time:

- Increased time to apply knowledge
- Increased time to utilize manipulatives
- Increased time to delve deeper with independent study

DIFFERENTIATION IN THE PRODUCT

Once material has been presented and the students have had opportunities to apply the instruction through practice and process, it is time to assess what they know. When I was a student myself, that meant taking a test, usually multiple choice. That meant lots of questions, lots of potential answers, and lots of reading. But that was…let's say more than several years ago! Times have changed; students have changed. And assessments need to change, too!

Some students enjoy giving a presentation and speaking in front of their classmates. Other students might be terrified by the thought of standing in front of everyone. For students who enjoy that, they will likely perform better than students who have more social anxiety and will probably receive a better grade, even though perhaps the student who didn't perform as well might know more about the topic.

When giving an assessment, it is important to note that grades should reflect what a student *knows*, *not* how good a student is at performing a certain task. That's true whether it's giving a presentation, writing with proper grammar and spelling, or even taking a test.

A good learning "product" will allow students to do these four things:

- Demonstrate their subject matter knowledge
- Allow them to apply their knowledge and understanding
- Think critically and creatively about a concept
- Reflect on what they have learned and relate it to what they already know

A good learning product will not:

- Be the same thing for every student

- Be the same type of product every time
- Measure how well a student can "take a test"

When it comes to differentiating the product, there are several stances teachers can take that ensure each student is able to really show what they know. One way is with a Product Menu. This might be called a "Homework Menu" or "Classwork Menu." Regardless of the name, it is essentially a choice board with options students can complete to demonstrate their ability and understanding.

When creating a product menu, make sure there are a variety of options that encompass many different expressive and learning styles. Students can choose a predetermined number of assignments or assessments to complete from the menu. This enables students to choose the products they will be best at. It also increases engagement and provides a sense of autonomy by giving students the opportunity to make the decision for themselves.

On a product menu, one option might be that students can create a short-form video like I used in my classroom. However, some students might not enjoy making a video and instead they might want to write a song or a report. Others still might prefer to be able to simply complete a worksheet (either online or on paper) as their assessment. The point of the menu is to allow students to express their knowledge in the way that lets them demonstrate

I can count to 20

Choose three tasks to complete to help you practice counting to 20!

Listen to a counting song and sing along.	Bounce a ball 20 times.	Draw 20 hearts and color them red.
Stand on one foot for 20 seconds.	Count 20 objects that you can find around your house (ex: candies, pasta noodles, etc)	Hop 20 times.
Make 20 dots with marker.	Do 20 jumping jacks.	Watch a short video about counting 1-20.

RebekahPoeTeaching

Example of a product menu where students need to select three of the activities to practice and demonstrate their ability to count to 20.

an ability to apply what they know to solve a problem or answer a question.

Another way to differentiate this is to raise or lower the number of required assignments or assessments that students must complete. Depending on the number of options you have, they might need to complete three in a row like tic tac toe or five in row like bingo. When having students choose more than one assignment, make sure the choices are all similar in the length of time and depth of knowledge required to complete them. Teachers might also allow students to complete assignments individually or with a group.

Back to my sixth graders—when we were trying to learn multiplication facts, I allowed them to pair up and gave each set of partners a number. Their assignment was to create a song that taught the multiplication facts for that number. They could change the lyrics to a current song or write something entirely original. Students were even allowed to look at songs that already existed for multiples of their number. The key was that the song had to be performed from memory. To differentiate this assignment even more, the students could choose whether they wanted to perform their song live or record it and play the video in class. And the songs they came up with or found varied widely. Some students rapped, another group sang a "Taylor Swift"-inspired country number, and another one went so far as to come up with choreography. I loved watching their creativity take over that project—which is not something I would have been able to see had I given them a typical worksheet.

Now don't get me wrong—we did plenty of worksheets and online drills, as well. But this broke up the monotony and let them express themselves a little bit more. I would go so far as to say it helped my sixth-grade class enjoy multiplication.

Differentiating the product not only lets students pick something they enjoy, it also helps students overcome their disabilities by allowing them to demonstrate their knowledge in the way that is easiest for them. Simply put, it provides them with the greatest chance for success.

For instance, for students with dysgraphia, a lengthy writing assignment is not likely going to give them the best chance for academic success, and is in fact likely to lead to anxiety and burn out. However, if they're instead allowed to give a monologue about a topic, they are still presenting the same information, but in a format that accommodates their disability.

The opposite might be true for a student with a speech or language impairment. They might do better writing an answer or choosing from multiple options rather than answering orally. The greatest thing to consider when creating and assigning an assessment is "Does this assessment allow my student to show what they know in the way that is best for them?" Remember, we are not assessing a student's ability to take a test; we are assessing how well they can apply what they have learned to develop a solution or come to a conclusion. And providing differentiated options for that product can help us do just that.

Differentiation in the Product
Demonstrate subject matter knowledge: • Focuses on what the student *knows*, not how well the student *tests* • Can take many forms
Apply new knowledge and activate prior knowledge: • Real-world scenarios • Project-based learning
Think critically and creatively: • Develop a song, skit, or presentation about a topic • Employ student interests to increase engagement

DIFFERENTIATION AND UNIVERSAL DESIGN FOR LEARNING

The Universal Design for Learning (UDL) has been around for much longer than you might think. It was developed by two researchers from the Harvard Graduate School of Education, Dr. David Rose and Dr. Ann Meyer. In 1984, they incorporated The Center for Applied Specialized Technology (CAST) in an effort to introduce technology that would customize learning experiences for students. Six years later, it shifted away from trying to be a solution to the struggles of the individual student and into a solution to common issues that were plaguing students school-wide. This shift mimicked what was being seen in other areas of society, as well.

Universal design was adopted as the architectural norm around the same time. People began realizing that what was designed to benefit one group of people actually benefited vastly more people than the target group. A common example of this is the "curb cut."

The "curb cut" was originally designed to benefit people who used wheelchairs. However, it benefited all. It turned out that everyone appreciated the flat transition from sidewalk to road, people pushing strollers or carts, people who used canes or walkers, even young children. It was a universally beneficial design.

So how does this tie into education? Much in the same way that a "curb cut" benefits everyone, the Universal Design for Learning (UDL) benefits all students by incorporating strategies and resources that make learning more ac-

cessible for everyone. With "one-size-fits-all" curricula, lessons and information are presented in one specific way. And by doing so, the lessons and information will likely not be accessible by all students.

If it's all print, students with reading difficulties will struggle to access the information being presented. Web-based programs rely on the fact that students can navigate technology, but that is not always the case. Likewise, it cannot be taken for granted that all students will even have access to technology.

UDL takes these considerations and provides solutions by providing multiple ways that students can understand, access, and reflect on the curriculum standards. Following UDL involves planning instruction that is accessible to all students, rather than focusing on individual needs. This approach reduces the need for frequent accommodations and removes unnecessary barriers in the learning process.UDL ensures that all students have equal access to the curriculum by focusing on three key curriculum areas: representation, action and expression, and engagement.

> **66**
> Universal Design for Learning is essentially the first step when it comes to differentiation.
> **99**

Differentiated instruction builds on the principles of a UDL curriculum. However, differentiation dives deeper to make sure that the curriculum is not only set up to be universally accessible, but that individual student learning needs are also met. Features of differentiated instruction can be interwoven within the guidelines laid out under UDL:

UDL Guideline	Feature of Differentiation
Multiple Means of Representation	• Material is provided as audio, video, or print to ensure accessibility • Use concrete manipulatives to illustrate abstract concepts • Provide models to demonstrate concepts
Multiple Means of Action and Expression	• Students can "show what they know" through multiple modalities • Consider varied deadlines or chunking assignments to assist students in tracking their progress • Regularly check for understanding through formative assessment
Multiple Means of Engagement	• Incorporate student interests and offer choice • Provide multiple options to access curricula • Relate concepts to prior knowledge

Universal Design for Learning is essentially the first step when it comes to differentiation because it sets up the curriculum to be accessible for all students without requiring constant modifications or retrofitting. Differentiation builds on UDL to make sure students as individuals can access the curriculum. However, when it comes to your students with IEPs, you will often have to go further. That's because you'll need to address not only the individual needs of the whole student, but those needs that are necessitated by their specific disabilities.

CHAPTER 8:
ACCOMMODATIONS & MODIFICATIONS

Understanding the nuanced difference between instructional strategies and accommodations is fundamental. It sets the stage for tailored, effective teaching. Navigating through its intricacies while delving into the art of selecting and seamlessly implementing accommodations can be tricky. However, it's an essential component of inclusive education. From addressing needs with instruction and assessment to ensuring accessibility across various learning environments and managing behavioral and sensory accommodations, educators can create truly inclusive spaces where students thrive.

> **Accommodations change the way a student accesses the curriculum based on their unique needs.**

As we discussed in the previous section, instructional strategies make the curriculum more accessible for all students. It helps increase understanding and offers different ways for students to express their knowledge. While similar to the purpose of accommodations, the two are not the same and are not interchangeable. It's a common belief that if a teacher is utilizing UDL guidelines and differentiating instruction then accommodations aren't needed.

However, that couldn't be further from the truth for students with disabilities. Further support and services that come through accommodations are crucial for these children. While instructional interventions and differentiated strategies address a skill or knowledge deficit, they do not address the specific barriers caused by disabilities. Accommodations change the way a student accesses the curriculum based on their unique needs. And just like differentiation, there are several areas where accommodations can be implemented.

Barrier	Universal Design for Learning	Differentiation	Accommodations
Language Barriers	Providing multiple means of representation, like visual aids, captions, and audio descriptions in materials.	Offering alternative readings or texts at varying reading levels based on students' proficiency.	Providing translations, interpreter services, or alternate assessments in the student's primary language.
Physical Accessibility	Using adjustable desks, providing wheelchair-accessible spaces, and incorporating assistive technologies for all students.	Offering varied activities allowing for different physical abilities and preferences.	Providing specific physical accommodations such as preferential seating or modified physical activities.
Learning Pace	Offering flexible timelines for completing assignments, allowing students to work at their own pace using multimedia resources.	Assigning tasks of varying complexities or depth based on students' readiness.	Allowing extended time for assignments or tests, providing audio versions of texts, or breaking tasks into smaller, manageable parts.
Sensory Overload	Incorporating options for noise reduction, providing visual schedules, and allowing for sensory breaks.	Offering alternative spaces or materials to reduce sensory stimuli.	Providing noise-canceling headphones, preferential seating, or a quiet area for focused work.
Executive Function Challenges	Providing visual organizers, checklists, and step-by-step instructions for tasks.	Allowing for varied methods of demonstrating understanding, such as presentations, projects, or written responses.	Offering extended time for completing tasks, allowing for frequent breaks, or providing additional prompts and cues for directions.

INSTRUCTION

What a student is learning does not change with accommodations. However, accommodations do change *how* a student learns. One such area where students might benefit from receiving accommodations is in the area of instruction.

In this area, accommodations change the way a student receives instruction and the resources that might be used during it. Sandra J. Thompson, Ph.D. offers four categories where instructional accommodations may take place. She states, "Accommodations are typically categorized according to whether they are changes in presentation, response, setting, or timing/scheduling."

Accommodations in the presentation of instruction increase its accessibility by incorporating non-traditional ways for students to be presented with new information. For example, students with a limited ability to gain information from printed text might require the use of an audio recording or video. Others may benefit from the use of printed notes with important information highlighted making it easier to locate. Accommodations in the instructional setting can also allow students to receive instruction in a smaller group with less distractions.

ASSESSMENT

Many accommodations used for instruction can also be used for assessment. Answering orally, hearing test questions read aloud, and cutting a long text into smaller sections can all be provided to students depending on their type of need. There are also some testing requirements that must be considered when providing accommodations on assessments, especially when it comes to state and standardized assessments.

Where I live in Alabama, students may receive accommodations on state assessments, but the types of available accommodations are limited. Typically, accommodations include the ability to test in a small group of ten or less, having extended time (up to double the standard allotted time), and the use of audio or "read aloud" services on certain portions of the test. The accommodations allowed for standardized assessments vary by state, so make sure you talk with your students' special education case managers or the building test coordinator to make sure your students are receiving the accommodations they need.

ACCESSIBILITY

When I taught sixth grade, I had three students for whom reading and writing was extremely difficult and negatively impacted the way they accessed the general education curriculum. It wasn't just in their ELA classes, but in science, social studies, and even math. In order to better allow them to access the information presented in the classroom and to relay what they knew, we utilized the built in accessibility features on their Chromebooks. They were able to highlight text on pdfs and web pages and have automated voices read the text aloud. Additionally, they could turn on a dictation feature and have their answers transcribed electronically.

These features were beneficial for my students in two ways. First, my students were able to better access the curriculum and the information they needed to learn in addition to responding to questions. The second benefit was the increased independence they gained. They did not need someone else to read to them or type their answers because the computer could do it. They didn't have to wait for me to have to sit next to them and do it on their behalf. This alleviated a lot of the stigma that can come from needing accommodations that can sometimes cause students to refuse help and not be as successful as they would be with them. With the increased use of technology in the classroom, accommodations for accessibility have become easier to implement than ever before.

BEHAVIORAL/SENSORY

For some students, there may be extenuating circumstances that contribute to a lack of academic progress or an inability to achieve successful outcomes in the general education setting. These students often have unique needs attributed to behavioral concerns or sensory needs. Accommodations can also be provided in these areas to help all students be successful in the general education classroom environment.

> We have to be willing to provide accommodations for students whose needs are less about academics and more about their interaction with the world around them.

Just like we as teachers must be willing to present information in a variety of ways and allow students to demonstrate their knowledge in the way that works best for them, we also have to be willing to provide accommodations for students whose needs are less about academics and more about their interaction with the world around them. Students with emotional disabilities, such as Autism, ADHD, emotional disturbance, and anxiety disorders to name a few, often have social interactions that appear different than the way neurotypical students interact within a setting. Too much distraction in an environment can negatively impact the way a student with ADHD is able to absorb new information, resulting in missing important steps and therefore an inability to perform a task or answer questions. For a student with autism, directions with too many steps can become confusing or even overwhelming. Students with emotional disabilities might struggle to manage their emotions appropriately and may "erupt" when angered. Accommodations can alleviate hindrances for these students tremendously.

For instance, a quieter environment for testing can help eliminate excess distractions and noise. Students may be allowed to take breaks during assignments instead of having to "push through" and get frustrated. Some children benefit from the use of noise canceling headphones. By providing accommodations for behavioral and sensory needs, teachers help students be successful in the classroom.

COMMON ACCOMMODATIONS

Instruction and Assessment	
Cutting assignments into smaller tasks	Peer helper
Color-coded questions and passages	Preferential seating
Concrete manipulatives (such as blocks)	Prompting to recall "next step"
Directions read aloud and repeated for clarity	Prompting to remain or return to task
	Providing "wait time" for students to answer/comply
Extended time to complete assessments	Reduced answer choices
Frequent checks for understanding	Reduced length of passages
Graphic organizer for note taking	Reduced number of problems given at a time
Lengthy tests chunked into sessions	Sentence stems
Multiplication chart	Small group testing location
Numbered paragraphs	Study guide given prior to test
Open book	Test materials read aloud
Open notes	Testing in native language
	Use of a calculator
	Visuals
	Word bank
Accessibility	**Behavioral/Sensory**
Assistive Technology	"Cool down" time
Audio files (eBooks)	Early class dismissal (to avoid crowded hallways)
Dictation-enabled devices	

Dictation to a scribe	First-Then strategies
Extra time to complete assignments	Minimizing distractions
High contrast materials	Noise-reduction headphones
Increased font size	Positive behavior supports
Increased opportunities to practice concepts	Prompting to remain on task
	Proximal seating
Increased wait time to allow for processing	Reduced visual clutter
	Reteaching in a small group setting
Multistep directions given one at a time	Token economy for rewards
	Sensory breaks
Noise-amplification system	Special lighting
Oral responses accepted	Visual schedule
Read-alouds by the teacher	
Simple, easy-to-read fonts	
Text-to-speech-enabled devices	
Translation device	

SELECTING AND IMPLEMENTING APPROPRIATE ACCOMMODATIONS

But how do you know what types of accommodations will benefit each student? Determining which accommodations to include in a student's IEP does not fall only to the special education teacher. Nor is it based solely on the parent's preference or through the general education teacher's feedback. Determining appropriate accommodations is the responsibility of the entire IEP team and is based on multiple factors including:

> **66** The first step to selecting appropriate accommodations is to discover what is causing a barrier to their learning in the first place. **99**

- Present levels of academic achievement and functional performance

- Individual strengths and needs

- Specific learning goals

- Academic or social behaviors that interfere with the student's learning

- Modalities (e.g., visual, auditory) that work best for the student

- Accommodations that have already been tried (what has and has not worked well)

- Some of the challenges presented by the use of these accommodations

- How the accommodation will be evaluated to determine whether it is working

- Whether the student is amenable to the accommodation and will likely use it (Iris Center, 2024)

The first step to selecting appropriate accommodations is to discover what is causing a barrier to their learning in the first place. In other words, in what ways is the student's disability hindering their academic performance. Knowing the barrier will allow the IEP team to determine which category the accommodations fall under.

SELECTING ACCOMMODATIONS

There are four main barriers to learning and as such there are four main categories of accommodations. The first is presentation. Barriers that impede the student's ability to understand presented information relate to the presentation category. These accommodations give the student a different way to access information. This might include adapting material to be accessed visually instead of auditorily or vice versa. The individual accommodation varies based on how students are best able to access the presented information.

For example, let's say we have a student named Jane who struggles with reading fluency. Perhaps Jane is spending so much time and effort simply trying to read the words that the meaning of the reading passage is completely lost to her. If that's the case, her disability is blocking her from retaining the information. That is the barrier, and she requires an accommodation to remove it. Jane would likely benefit from being able to listen to passages as audio files as a way to process the information being presented.

Let's consider another student, who we'll call Thomas. Thomas can read at grade level, yet he becomes fatigued and overwhelmed when given lengthy passages, so he makes errors when answering comprehension questions due to his disability. For Thomas, an accommodation could be to cut the text into smaller sections and have him answer questions about one section of text at a time. In both instances, accommodations are being made to the way that information is presented to the students.

Another category of accommodations is response. These accommodations change the way students are required to respond to learned information, i.e. class assignments, homework, and assessments. Students with disabilities that affect their ability to produce written work, whether due to physical limitations or dysgraphia, are not able to provide written answers. Without an alternate way for them to show what they know, their disability receives a poor grade instead of reflecting their level of knowledge. They would benefit from utilizing talk-to-text features, a scribe, or sentence stems.

Conversely, some students struggle with issues due to a speech-language impairment. For these students, the opposite might be true. They might need to be able to write or type out answers instead of answering orally. Providing accommodations in student response ensures that teachers are collecting data on what a student knows—not on how a student performs.

Other accommodations may be related to the setting or to timing. Accommodations to the setting include making arrangements for a student to test in a small group setting or individually. It includes considerations like desk placement (sitting closer to the teacher, away from windows to eliminate distractions, etc.). It could also include different lighting. In years past, I covered my classroom's fluorescent lights with thin material to reduce the bulbs' intensity for my students who needed a calmer environment.

For accommodations related to timing, extended time to complete an assignment or assessment can help students who need more time to process information and understand what a question is asking. Even a teacher simply letting more time pass between when a question is asked and an answer is given can allow the student time to process what's being asked in order to answer or comply.

After the IEP team determines the barrier to the student's learning, it is time to select accommodations. They are entirely dependent on the individual needs of different students. Again, this is not based on opinion. It is something that a general education teacher needs to weigh in on, because they will often spend significantly more time with special education students than the special education case managers. This is why it's imperative that data from the general education teacher is utilized in the development of the IEP.

In my career, any time it grew closer to the time for a student to have a new IEP, I sent out Google forms to my general education teacher counterparts. The forms asked specific questions about the student's performance in their class.

As the case manager, I wanted to know:

- What interventions and accommodations has the student been receiving in the general education classroom?

- Have those been making a positive difference?

- Do any of the accommodations need to be amended? If so, what data do you have to quantify that decision?

- What areas of learning seem to be the student's biggest struggle?

- What areas of learning seem to be the student's strong suit?

There were so many other things as well. Through the information gathered from the general education teacher, I could make sure that the accommodations going into the IEP were ones that the student truly needed.

IMPLEMENTING ACCOMMODATIONS

When it comes to implementing accommodations in the general education classroom, teachers often want to provide students with everything they need, but many are at a loss as to how to do it.

In a 2021 study, general education teachers listed common barriers to providing accommodations. They included a lack of communication with special education teachers, limited time in class in which to provide the accommodations, and a lack of understanding about the accommodations themselves. If that is the case, how can general education teachers be and feel more successful when implementing accommodations?

As we discussed earlier, collaboration between special education teachers and general education teachers is essential to providing students with the necessary support to be as successful as possible. This includes asking for additional help or support.

As a resource teacher, I gave out copies of IEPs along with shorter "IEP at-a-glance" forms at the beginning of every school year before students returned to classrooms. This helped my general education teachers familiarize themselves with the purpose and practice of the accommodation, and if they needed more information, by asking questions or for examples.

Once the school year starts, teachers hit the ground running, and time is definitely a concern. Something that helps is finding ways accommodations can be made in advance. For example, my third-grade teachers used the same curriculum year after year. Rather than making accommodations to individual assignments or assessments on our own, we got together and made them as a team. That way, things were ready to go at the beginning of the year. It took a little time at the front end, but we were able to save time in the long run.

Occasionally, students may refuse an accommodation, as is their right. If a student is refusing an accommodation, the first thing to do is to figure out why. Is it that the student feels they do not need it? Does the student not know how to use it? Is the student embarrassed to use it? Either way, an accommodation that is not being used is not helping to support the student. In that instance, discuss it with the student's special education case manager to problem-solve.

Sometimes, a student might not understand how to use an accommodation. If they are given manipulatives for solving math equations, they require instruction in the use of those manipulatives. Teachers will not be able to determine if the manipulatives are effective if the student uses them improperly.

A common accommodation that has been made more prevalent in recent years is the use of a fidget tool for students with ADHD or children who need sensory input to increase their ability to focus. While these tools can be effective, if used incorrectly, they can cause even more of a distraction. Implementing fidget tools as an accommodation requires instruction for the student on how to use it in a way that will benefit them instead of in a way that is more like play.

When I worked with a former student who I will call Eric, I knew he would benefit from a fidget tool. He was constantly squirming, rolling his pencil around his desk instead of doing his work, etc. Had I simply handed him a fidget tool, he would have played with it. Instead, we had a whole class discussion about how we can use different tools in the classroom for different purposes, and that some students needed different tools than others. We devised expectations for the use of these fidget tools, and I provided explicit instruction and modeled how they should be used.

Eric learned he preferred to use a "spinner" as well as when using the spinner benefitted him most: during circle time and while completing independent work. He would pull it from his supply box, place it on his desk, and spin it with one hand while the other was writing on his paper or listening to our morning circle meeting. Using this tool helped decrease his off-task behavior and increase his ability to participate and pay attention.

If a student is not wanting to use an accommodation because they are embarrassed, brainstorm some ways that the same result can be met in a less obvious way. For example, I once had a student who was embarrassed to raise his hand to ask questions because, in his words, "None of the other kids have to do that." He was embarrassed to reveal that he did not understand what the teacher was saying, so instead of asking for clarification, he went along in confusion. To alleviate his embarrassment, we devised a smaller signal to show the teacher he needed additional assistance that wasn't as visible as raising his hand. When he used the signal, Eric's teacher knew that he needed more help and was able to provide it.

Some students might not want to accept certain accommodations, like having a test read aloud, because having to go to another room with a different teacher to take their test would be an obvious difference from their nondisabled peers. One way to alleviate that is with technology. With the advancements and accessibility features that are now available in most schools, students can remain in their classes and listen to tests read aloud on their computers or other devices. There are ways that accommodations can be encouraged and modified so that students are more likely to use them.

Being familiar with modern tech and specialized equipment can help teachers in implementing accommodations. With automatic features like spell check, students who struggle with spelling and writing are able to overcome that struggle. Additionally, many devices contain built-in accessibility features that support usage. From text-to-speech and dictation features to automated captions in videos, these features can add to accommodations within the classroom. Other extensions can also help, such as plug-ins or sites that change the size of fonts, descriptive screen reading, or even remove distractions from webpages.

EVALUATING ACCOMMODATIONS

Once you know the barrier to your students' learning and have selected and implemented the accommodations needed to promote their academic success, how do you know if an accommodation is working or not? Dr. Marty Beech of Florida State University lists four questions that must be answered to determine the effectiveness of an accommodation.

First, you'll need to ask, did the student regularly use the accommodation? Comparing how many times it was offered to how many times the accommodation was used can play a large role in determining if it's truly needed.

Second, ask yourself: did the accommodation allow the student to participate fully in the activity to the same degree as their nondisabled peers? Remember, accommodations do not change the requirements of a standard; they make it so the standard can be equitably accessed, understood, and learned.

Thirdly, ask, was the student able to make sufficient progress in meeting the grade-level standards with the accommodation? If we have a student with a reading disability, and we begin providing an accommodation where the student's test is read aloud to him, we would want to see test grades begin to improve. If they are not improving, that shows there is more preventing the student from being successful than an inability to accurately read test passages and questions. However, if we are seeing the grades improve, we know the accommodation is sufficient.

> **Just because a student starts the year off with a certain accommodation in place does not mean that accommodation must stay all year.**

The last question is, did the accommodation enable the student to feel like they were truly part of the class? Remember, for education to truly be inclusive, students must truly feel *included*. They should be part of group projects and partner work, but should also be able to have conversations with peers and feel part of a friend group. In other words, it is not enough for students to simply be taught alongside their classmates. They must be fully integrated into the classroom experience.

If the answer to any of these four questions is a "no," it's up to the IEP team to determine where the accommodation has fallen short and devise a new one to take its place. Accommodations can be flexible; just because a student starts the year off with a certain accommodation in place does not mean that accommodation must stay all year. They can be changed, removed, or added to provide the student with the support they need to not only be academically successful, but also to be a fully included member of the class.

MAKING MODIFICATIONS

If accommodations are changes made to the way the students access the curriculum, modifications are changes made to the curriculum itself. I've met many teachers, parents, administrators, etc. who use the terms "accommodations" and "modifications" interchangeably, as if they were the same thing. While the terms are similar, they are not the same, they do not serve the same function, and they cannot be used interchangeably.

DIFFERENTIATION VERSUS ACCOMMODATIONS VERSUS MODIFICATIONS

So how can you remember or explain the difference between the terms? As a foodie, I like to explain the difference between these three terms in reference to food—in particular, a nice, juicy steak.

Let me set the scene (I'd tell you to close your eyes, but you're reading this, so that won't work). Imagine you are a waiter at a fancy restaurant. The restaurant is filled with hungry patrons, and the special of the night is a cut of ribeye steak. Some of the guests prefer their steaks cooked medium-rare while some enjoy medium-well. Some use steak sauce and some don't. There are a few guests, however, for whom a whole ribeye steak is too difficult to eat. So for those guests, you tell the chef to cut the steak into thin strips for fajitas or turn the steak into ground meat and make hamburger patties or meatballs. And there are a very small number of guests who can't eat steak at all, so they get a chicken dish instead. Each guest gets what they need, and each is satisfied with a full belly at the end of the meal.

And now that we're all hungry and craving a fancy dinner, let's consider how a quality steak is similar to a quality curriculum. The steak is the same from patron to patron, just as the core curriculum is the same from student to student. The way the steak is cooked, however, whether it is medium rare or well done, or perhaps whether steak sauce is used, represents differentiation. The steak isn't altered very much. Subtle changes can be done fairly easily and customized for each person.

Slicing or grinding the steak represents accommodations. The steak is presented differently, but it is still the same piece of steak, just like how the same standards are being taught in the classroom, perhaps just in a different way or with a greater amount of support to make the curriculum easier to access.

Finally, we get to the customers who receive a chicken dish. This represents modification. The dish is entirely different, just like a modified curriculum is different. It is not the same level of difficulty, not the same grade-level at times, nor is it the same standard being learned as the rest of the class.

Let's say we have a fifth-grade class working on multi-digit multiplication. To differentiate the lesson, you might have some students working in small groups on different tasks or playing games. They might be completing different types of assignments. For students who need accommodations, they might use manipulatives or a multiplication chart or have the steps written out on a note so they can remember the sequence. Modifications, however, would be students who are not working on multiplication at all. They would have alternate assignments that cover different standards—perhaps they're working on double digit addition and subtraction instead.

WHEN ARE MODIFICATIONS APPROPRIATE?

Personally, I have only ever utilized program modifications with one student who I will call Melvin, a first grader with significant classroom behavior struggles. The student was missing several prerequisite skills which made the first-grade standards very difficult for him. Melvin would get frustrated and stop paying attention and attempt to run around the room or out the door. Sometimes, he'd throw his papers and pencils at his peers and teachers. His behavior played a large factor in the decision to place him on a modified curriculum temporarily. Instead of working on the same assignments as his typical peers, we gave Melvin activities at his level that he enjoyed so we could teach the behavior skills he needed such as attending to a task, following directions, and participating with the class.

This was not a decision I made alone; this was an IEP team decision agreed upon by every single member of the team. We agreed to take nine weeks to modify the curriculum in an effort to focus most of the instruction on his behavior and on learning those prerequisite skills that would enable him to eventually make progress in the general education curriculum. After those nine weeks, we would reassess and either extend or end the modification.

One major factor that influenced the decision to modify Melvin's curriculum was the fact that he was only in the first grade. As students enter secondary grades, they have to earn required credits to meet graduation requirements. Students who are on a modified curriculum are not earning credits for classes because they aren't learning the required grade level standards necessary for a diploma. Because of this, I strongly recommend thinking deeply and trying everything before modifying a curriculum for an older student.

Note that students who are on alternate standards, such as those in self-contained special education classrooms, are not actually receiving modifications. They are utilizing an entirely separate set of standards that have been specially developed to meet their unique needs and fulfill the specific demands of that type of classroom. And as they are a separate set of standards, they are not considered a modification, but rather a separate curriculum.

Accommodations and modifications should be added or removed after careful consideration, based on student need, ability, and corresponding data. The inclusion of these in a student's IEP is a team-based decision. Remember, the goal is to create an inclusive classroom where every student has the opportunity to succeed, and understanding accommodations and modifications will help you feel more confident about tailoring your teaching strategies to meet the diverse needs of your students.

CHAPTER 9:
MULTISENSORY INSTRUCTIONAL APPROACHES

Multisensory learning combines strategies that engage various senses in the learning process to enhance understanding, retention, and participation. By weaving together auditory, visual, tactile, and kinesthetic elements, we can create immersive learning experiences that cater to the unique abilities of all students.

WHAT IS MULTISENSORY LEARNING?

Multisensory learning is defined as "process of learning a new subject matter through the use of two or more senses. This may include combining visual, auditory, tactile or kinaesthetic, olfactory and gustatory sensation" (Prasana, 2018). Studies show that when taught a new subject through the use of multiple modalities, information is learned faster and retained longer (Neumann, et al.). This is likely because we are used to existing in a multisensory world.

For example, let's say we are watching a horse race. We see the horses running, hear their hooves stomping, and feel the air as they rush by. We smell all the smells associated with horses. All those sensations together are what make up a horse race. It makes sense then that our instruction of new material should encompass and engage multiple senses congruently for students to have a full experience and learn to the best of their abilities.

MULTISENSORY LEARNING VERSUS LEARNING STYLES

While it is useful to utilize a multisensory approach when teaching all students, it becomes essential when teaching students with disabilities. Studies show that, when teaching students with disabilities, multisensory learning strategies give each student the opportunity to foster their learning abilities in other areas by reducing the cognitive load through presenting information in more than one modality.

So let's talk about "learning styles" for a minute. I remember being in school myself and taking a "learning style" quiz. It had questions like, "Would you rather read a book or listen to music?" And at the end, based on a very few simple questions, it said if you were a visual learner, an auditory learner, or a kinesthetic learner.

However, the whole idea of "learning styles" is a neuromyth—"a misconception generated by a misunderstanding of scientifically established facts (by brain research) to make a case for the use of brain research in education and other contexts" (OECD, 2002). The problem with those labels is that they pigeonhole students and teachers into thinking students can only learn when that style is utilized or that every student is able to learn "well" if information is presented in their style.

As an example, I want to tell you a story about my husband, Andrew. He is a middle school band director (bless his heart), and highly educated and intelligent. But if you ask him about reading, he will tell you he hates reading. He will tell you how bad he is at reading. All his life, he has been told by teachers and online quizzes that he is an auditory learner who struggles to comprehend written material, and as such, cannot learn information just from reading it.

> **When learning takes place, the physical structure of the brain changes.**

Contrary to his opinion, however, the man reads all the time. He reads online articles about topics he is interested in. He reads graphic novels and comics and can tell you anything you want to know (or don't want to know) about anything he's read. He can read and read well, so it's not that he *can't* read to comprehend, it's that he *assumes* he cannot, and therefore doesn't try.

I can pretty much guarantee you that you have a "Little Andrew" in your class, a student who thinks reading for information is beyond their capacity because they are an "auditory learner" or a "kinesthetic learner." And if we as teachers allow those beliefs to proliferate, we are not empowering our students to learn to the best of their abilities.

Instead of focusing on one modality as a "learning style," it is essential to understand how the brain learns new information. When learning takes place, the physical structure of the brain changes.

Studies show that:

"Learning appears to occur primarily because of changes in the strength and number of the connections between existing neurons, a process called *synaptic plasticity*. For the most part, the changes occur in such a way that frequently used connections between neurons are enhanced the most" (Quak, London, & Talsma, 2015).

In other words, "Practice makes perfect." The more connections are used, the stronger they become.

In the summer of 2023, I attended a professional development session by Dr. Shane Saeed, and she used a brilliant metaphor to help attendees understand synaptic plasticity. She said to think of neural pathways in the same way you think of making a path in a forest. The first time you try to make a path, the branches are in the way. Leaves cover the ground making it hard to distinguish. But over time, the more the pathway is used, it starts to become easier to see and navigate. The plants underfoot become trampled and the dirt is hard packed by repeated treks. Eventually, a trail is formed that is simple to follow. With repeated use of neural pathways, the connection grows stronger and retaining and recalling that information becomes easier.

BENEFITS OF MULTISENSORY LEARNING FOR STUDENTS WITH DISABILITIES

As I mentioned, our brains are designed to understand and interact with our environment using multiple modalities. Our ability to do so often depends on using multiple sensory channels simultaneously, even when the learning material is designed for a single sense.

According to research, "an important benefit of multisensory learning is its use of 'dual coding', which 'reduces cognitive load because information from different modalities can be more easily chunked into short-term memory and used to build long term representations'" (Fadeev and Milyakina, 2020). Essentially, as multiple modalities are used, more neural pathways form across different parts of the brain, allowing for information to be learned faster and retained longer.

Multisensory instruction also provides students with an increased opportunity to make connections to prior knowledge. For example, a student learning what an octagon is by examining the shape will likely be able to relate it to a stop sign—something that is common in the student's environment.

Researchers investigated the effects of multisensory instruction on recall when that instruction was paired with participants' pre-existing knowledge. As you might imagine, they found that participants who were able to activate prior knowledge through the use of multisensory instruction had greater memory performance than those for whom prior knowledge was not utilized.

Activating prior knowledge also helps students not have to rely so heavily on working memory when it comes to recalling information. It is estimated that 20%-50% of students with disabilities such as ADHD, learning disabilities, cognitive impairments, and language deficits have a poor working memory. When multiple modalities are utilized in instruction, simultaneous yet independent processing occurs across different areas of the brain.

A 2009 study revealed that participants who were shown either pictures with accompanying environmental sounds (such as a picture of a cat and an audio recording of a cat meowing) or written words accompanied by the word spoken aloud had a higher recall rate versus participants who were only shown the picture or word. The study concluded that higher recall rate was due in part to the utilization of long-term memory associations paired with working memory (Quak, London, & Tilsma, 2015).

For students with disabilities, a multisensory experience across all subject areas gives students the greatest opportunity for successful learning. In the area of mathematics, the use of multisensory instruction makes abstract concepts more concrete.

I once taught a third grader who was able to rote count to 100 easily. But if I asked him to give me ten blocks? He couldn't do it. He would count by rote until he got to ten, handing me however many blocks one at a time. And he counted quickly. So he might say "ten" but only actually separate three blocks from the rest. He struggled with the concept that the first block was "one" and that each consecutive block constituted two, three, and so on. I worked with him on this by having him not say the next number until he touched the next block. I also used a tens frame and showed him that each square of the frame needed one block. I even numbered the squares. His instruction used auditory (counting aloud), visual (seeing the tens frame and numbers), and kinesthetic modalities (touching each block one at a time) to help him conceptualize 1:1 correspondence.

> **Even when the subject matter is unisensory, we can (and should) use multiple modalities in our instruction.**

And these results are not happenstance. There is research that backs it up. According to studies conducted in 2019, students who had the opportunity to utilize physical materials (versus no materials in one study and pictorial representations in the other) had a greater number of correct solutions and demonstrated the use of more conceptually developed strategies to find those solutions (Pires, et. al., 2019).

But the benefits of physical materials and manipulatives are not confined only to the area of mathematics. Even when the subject matter is unisensory, we can (and should) use multiple modalities in our instruction. When it comes to reading, we often think of it as a unisensory experience. After all, aren't we only looking at words on a page?

However, in a 2004 study, Neuman and his team of researchers found that a group of preschool students who explored letters using 3-D foam letters had a better understanding of the alphabetic principle and decoding skills than two other groups. The second group of students had been shown letters printed on paper and glued to a board and the third group had been shown letters on a computer screen. But the first group with the 3-D foam letters surpassed them both.

Researchers Neuman, Hyde, Neuman, et al state:

> "[Studies have shown that] Adding tactile and kinaesthetic stimulation may make the connections between letters and sounds easier to learn and, thereby, improve decoding skills. They also suggested that using tactile-kinaesthetic exploration activities in early literacy programs may encourage young children to process letters in a more investigative way, something they would probably not do spontaneously if letters were presented only in visual form."

In all instruction, the evidence shows that when students use multiple modalities when learning new material, they demonstrate better results.

STRATEGIES FOR INCORPORATING MULTISENSORY APPROACHES INTO LESSONS

Adding multisensory instruction to your lessons doesn't have to be a big production. With just a few well-thought-out strategies and materials, you can begin incorporating multiple modalities into every lesson. And finding materials doesn't have to break the bank. Chances are you already have materials in your classroom, and a few additional items can take your lessons to the next level.

Here are a few of my favorite materials and ideas to use when creating lessons that incorporate multisensory instruction.

Ideas for Multisensory Instruction in Phonological Awareness	
Material	**Use**
Rubber bands	Use these to stretch out the sounds in a word. Students will hold a rubber band and stretch it slightly every time they say a letter sound in a CVC word. When they release the tension on the rubber band, they will say the word.

Play-Doh	Play-Doh can be used in so many ways in your reading instruction. Students can form the shapes of letters with their Play-Doh or use letter stamps to stamp the shape of the letter into the dough. They can form balls of dough and squish one ball for each sound they hear in a CVC word.
Sandpaper	Students can trace letter shapes on the sandpaper with their fingers. They can also put the sandpaper underneath a sheet of regular paper and write their letters with crayons. The added bumps from the sandpaper add an additional tactile sensation and once the sandpaper is removed, the crayon markings will remain slightly textured so children can trace the letters with their fingers.
Cinnamon Sticks (check for allergies)	Students can use the cinnamon sticks to write letter shapes on the sandpaper. This will stimulate the olfactory system to add an additional modality to the activity.
Mega Bloks	Did you know you can write on plastic Mega Bloks with a dry erase marker? It's a game changer; am I right? Write words on the blocks with three or more prongs (making sure there is one sound per prong). Write letters (or digraphs) on blocks with one prong. Students can use the individual blocks to build the words on the multi-prong blocks. You can also write letters/digraphs and vowels to build and read words in the same word family.
Shaving Cream or Sand Trays	Did you ever write in shaving cream as a young student? I distinctly remember doing this in elementary school, and it was one of my favorite activities. You can call out words or letter names/sounds to the students, and they can spell them out by writing in the shaving cream. You can also use sand trays for these activities, but be warned: it might get everywhere.

3-D Letters	There are *many* types of 3-D letters made from different materials. I really liked using letters that were magnetic because they would stick to my classroom whiteboard for whole group activities or a magnetic board that I kept at my small group table. Students can explore these letters by tracing the edges and surfaces. They can also manually move the letters to build words or match sounds.
Pop-its	I don't know about you, but at one point the entire school where I taught was overrun with pop-its! The students were completely obsessed. And if you can't beat them, you might as well join them! Use the bubbles on the pop-its to represent letter sounds: have students "pop" one of the bubbles for each sound or syllable in a word.
Hands and fingers	No resources? No problem! Students can tap out sounds or letters in a word with their fingers on their desk or with their hands on their arms. They can clap out sounds or syllables in a word. They can "write" letters in the air with their fingers. And the best part about using this as a multisensory resource? Nothing to clean up at the end of the lesson!

Ideas for Multisensory Instruction in Math	
Material	**Use**
Puzzles	When I had students who were working on counting to 100, I used a 100-piece puzzle with the numbers 1-100 written on each piece in rows. Students would build the puzzles, saying the correct numbers in order as they built it. This was a favorite activity of several members of my class, and the repetition and putting the pieces together while seeing the numbers helped them learn to count to 100 quite quickly.

Linking Cubes	Linking cubes are a great way to visualize addition and subtraction. For subtraction, students can start with a stack of linked cubes representing the minuend (the number you start with). Then, they can remove the number of cubes that represent the subtrahend (the number being subtracted). They'll be left with the difference. For addition, students can make two stacks of cubes to represent the addends, then attach and count them together to get the sum.
Tens Frames	Students can use tens frames to work on counting with 1:1 correspondence. They can also use them when working on very simple addition and subtraction problems. Students can put one small item into each square, or if it is dry erase or paper, draw a dot or write the number inside the squares.
Blocks or Tokens	Students can represent numbers with blocks or tokens. They can also use them to "count on" from a number when it comes to addition. Start with the first addend written in its numerical form. Use blocks to represent the second addend. If there is an addition problem of 5+3, students can say "5" and then "count on" with the three blocks: 5, 6, 7, 8. This is an important skill to have so they don't have to always start at "1" when adding or counting.
Play-Doh	Students can create numbers out of Play-Doh or use number stamps and trace the imprint they made. They can also pull off pieces of Play-Doh to represent a given number.
Base Ten Blocks	These are *great* to use when you are working on double digit addition and subtraction or higher. Students can see and touch the blocks to see how ten "ones" is the same as one "ten" by exchanging them for one another in a math problem. They can also make 100 blocks that are represented by 10x10 squares and 1000 blocks that are represented by 10x10x10 cubes.

Number Line	Number lines come in all sizes. I've used small ones that students could use with their fingers to move from number to number. I even used to have one that stretched across the floor. My students used it by jumping from number to number. A number line can help make the concept of "negative numbers" make more sense, especially when trying to understand why a -7 is a "smaller number" than -2.
Pop-its	Again, pop-its can come in handy! Students can use these to work on counting with 1:1 correspondence by "popping" one bubble for each number. They can also use them for "counting on." Your class can even use them for simple addition or subtraction problems.
Fingers	I am of the firm belief that counting on your fingers is an appropriate strategy for anyone at any level. Whether it is skip counting, addition, subtraction, or counting with 1:1 correspondence… so many math concepts can be strengthened simply by using your fingers.
3-D Shapes	When students are trying to learn to recognize and name shapes, 3-D representations come in handy. Children can trace and count edges of 2-D shapes like squares, triangles, and edges, or faces of 3-D shapes like cubes and pyramids.

Other Ideas for Multisensory Instruction—No physical materials necessary!	
Strategy	**Use**
Music/Videos/ Choreography	Using songs and motions is a great way to learn! There are fantastic videos on YouTube that play songs that teach everything from skip counting and order of operations to the water cycle and the preamble of the constitution. And some of the tunes are *catchy*, so don't be surprised if you or your students start singing them randomly throughout the day.

Acting	For students who are struggling with reading comprehension, acting out what they are reading can help make the story come to life. Some students struggle with visualizing what's happening in a story just by reading the words, so pairing that with the visual and physical representation of the story can help it make more sense and improve the student's recall. For vocabulary terms, students can even act out the definition in a game of charades!
Virtual Field Trips	There are many museums, galleries, and nature preserves that offer "virtual field trips" online. Instead of just reading about an eagle's nest, students can watch a live stream of a mama eagle taking care of her eggs. You can even use features like Google Earth to show students historical buildings in an almost 3-D depiction instead of just a picture in a textbook.

While all students will benefit from multisensory instruction, utilizing multiple modalities in your strategies and interventions allows students with disabilities to use their strengths in different areas. It gives them the opportunity to learn in the way that works best for them. After all, it is our goal as educators to make learning a vibrant, interactive journey for every student. By engaging multiple senses, we create richer, more dynamic learning experiences that can help all students connect with the material in meaningful ways.

CHAPTER 10:
ASSESSING PROGRESS AND
MONITORING IEP GOALS

Understanding what and how to teach students with disabilities is an essential part of creating an inclusive classroom environment. But how do you know if the way you're teaching is working or if it needs to be adjusted? How can you accurately assess student progress toward their IEP goals, not to mention accommodations? How do you know if they're appropriate or if you need to add or remove them from the IEP? That's where progress monitoring comes in.

Progress monitoring "occurs throughout the data-based individualization (DBI) process to assess responsiveness to the validated intervention platform, as well as adaptations to the intervention" (IntensiveIntervention.org, 2024). When it comes to progress monitoring, you've got three big decisions to make:

What method will you use to monitor progress? The type of goal you're tracking is going to determine what method you'll utilize. I can't collect progress monitoring data on a behavior goal with work samples. The method used to collect the data depends on the goal.

How often are you going to conduct progress monitoring? That's going to be different for the types of goals. You want to make sure you're monitoring closely enough to determine effectiveness, but not so close that you can't see improvement.

How will you collect progress monitoring data? This is different from the method you'll use. Method is more of what you'll get from the student and collecting is what you are going to do as the teacher. And we're going to go over each of those questions in more detail.

WHAT METHOD WILL YOU USE FOR PROGRESS MONITORING?

When I was a first-year teacher, I loved a worksheet. I think it's because that's how I grew up. As a child of the 90s and early 2000s, every assignment I did in class was a paper/pencil worksheet. And when I was student teaching, that's what the teacher I did my student teaching under loved. One plus for this method is that it's a concrete piece of evidence and data. However, I learned in my decade-plus of experience that there is more to data collection. There are some goals wherein a worksheet simply isn't going to help.

Let's first talk about the situations and goals where a worksheet might be a good option. Let's say I want to collect a work sample with a worksheet because I'm assessing math fluency—addition, subtraction, etc. I will also likely want to use one for a writing assignment, handwriting, and things of that nature. Reading comprehension is also a good subject for a worksheet style assessment where students need to highlight text evidence to show how they came up with their answer. Anywhere you need to see the thought process like showing your work in a multi-step math problem, a worksheet might be a good option.

Another option for data collection are student assessments. I like to use assessments when I'm still collecting academic data, but it's more of a mental process like reading fluency or decoding. Counting to 100 or something like that can't really be done with a worksheet. It's something I need to hear the students doing to take accurate data.

The images shown below are examples of student assessment sheets I created. It shows pages with letters in random order that the student and I would each have a copy of. The student would identify the letters on their pages while I marked the letters identified correctly or incorrectly on my copy. For these, I laminated the student versions so I could reuse them. I made one copy of the teacher version for each student, and those were the pages I saved to use for

Letter Identification

lowercase letters

q	o	n	i	e	y
c	k	p	z	u	m
s	r	d	w	v	t
j	g	b	x	a	l
f	h				

UPPERCASE LETTERS

J	O	N	S	M	Y
T	V	K	A	P	Z
E	G	B	U	F	X
Q	W	I	C	H	R
L	D				

@lessons_and_lattes 2022

Letter Sounds

consonant sounds

q	s	f	l	r	n
d	v	w	z	hard C	soft C
b	h	p	t	j	k
y	m	hard g	soft g		

vowel sounds

long	a	e	i	o	u
short	a	e	i	o	u

long vowel teams

ee	ay	oa	ai	ea
ue	oi	ey	oe	oy

r-controlled vowels

ir	ar	er	ur	or

@lessons_and_lattes 2022

progress monitoring.

For more abstract concepts, a teacher observation is going to be your best bet. This will include collecting data on social and emotional skills, peer-to-peer interactions, and functional skills. You're going to watch and see what the student does. The length of the observation will depend on the type of observation and what you are looking for. If I am observing that a student can stay on task during a lesson, I'll watch for the whole lesson. If I am watching to see how a student interacts with his peers on the playground, 20-30 minutes will usually suffice.

Phonemic Awareness Assessment Name_____ Date_____

Lowercase Letter Names

q o n i e y c k p z u m s r d w v t j g b x a l f h

___/26

Uppercase Letter Names

J O N S M Y T V K A P Z E G B U F X Q W I C H R L D

___/26

Consonant Sounds

q s f l r n d v w z c b h p t j k y x m g   (hard/soft)

(hard/soft)

___/23

Vowel Sounds

a e i o u

___/5 (long) ___/5 (short)

I can imagine you asking, "How am I supposed to observe a student for 30 minutes when I have 20 other students I have to teach?" That goes back to the collaboration we discussed earlier in the book. You cannot do this alone.

When I was co-teaching, I would dedicate specific days to collecting data and doing observations (this is a time when the "One Teach; One Observe" model of co-teaching is appropriate). During that time, my co-teacher would teach the subject matter and I would dedicate my time to observing specific students. I typically only had to conduct such a long observation if it was time for the student's three-year reevaluation or their initial eligibility evaluation. Otherwise, I might observe for a shorter amount of time and then get back into teaching.

HOW OFTEN ARE YOU GOING TO CONDUCT PROGRESS MONITORING?

Perhaps you find yourself asking, "How on earth am I supposed to do this and how often should it be?'" And again, say it with me now…"It depends on the goal!" Are you catching the theme yet? Data collection is determined by what you're collecting data on, and just like the method you use might change based on the goal, the frequency of progress monitoring is going to change as well.

Let's travel back in time and meet up with "first-year-teacher" me. First year teacher Mrs. Poe would probably not talk to you because she'd be elbows deep in data and feeling like she needed to be progress monitoring every day. That's right. I had my data collection binder and I was making notes every single day. Of course, I was wondering why the kids and I were stressed out and why I wasn't seeing the progress I wanted. It's because all I was really doing was assessing. Solely focused on trying to see improvement, I was neglecting the other necessary aspects of teaching. I was so focused on getting the output I wanted, I wasn't giving the students the input they needed.

To make a long story short, it didn't work. So, I talked with my mentor teacher, and we came up with a better schedule based on the students' goals. Once I implemented that schedule, I began to see steady improvement in my students' performance.

For academic goals, the most often I would recommend collecting data for progress monitoring is once a week. You could collect weekly data on things like math fact fluency, spelling, counting and bi-weekly/twice a month for things that take a little longer to practice and learn—things like decoding in reading. In that instance, you would want to wait a couple of weeks between progress monitoring sessions for decoding CVC words. Monthly progress monitoring is going to be an area that takes much more time to actually see any progress. Reading fluency is one area that sticks out. You're not likely to see a big change in reading fluency each week, but compared to the month before, you are probably going to see a pretty good jump.

> **I was so focused on getting the output I wanted, I wasn't giving the students the input they needed.**

For behavior goals, that's going to be a little different because often you'll be collecting data as the behavior occurs or does not occur. In 2021, I had a student who I will call Carrie, who had a behavior goal to choose a non-violent option for dealing with conflict. To meet her goal, she had to go a full nine weeks without getting into a physical altercation. Initially, I noted data each day with a + or - depending on if she physically engaged in conflict with a peer. Once she was able to go a week without fighting, I tracked data weekly. At the end of each week, if she hadn't fought, I made a note reflecting that. If there were days where she did fight, that data was collected immediately with notes being written the same day.

The good news is that Carrie did meet that goal. She got to the point where she'd find me and tell me how many days there'd been without a fight. She was so proud of herself. And Carrie would tell her friends not to get her involved in their mess because she wasn't a fighter anymore. I can honestly say it was one of the highlights of my whole year.

When it comes to determining how often to conduct progress monitoring, you will look at your students' goals and determine the frequency needed to collect data. Behavior data is dependent on the behavior occurring or not. For academic goals, anywhere from weekly to monthly can be appropriate depending on the skills being assessed. This leads us to the next step, which is how we'll collect the needed data.

HOW WILL YOU COLLECT PROGRESS MONITORING DATA?

Now like I said, the method you use for progress monitoring depends on what you are getting from the student. How you are collecting that data, on the other hand, has to do with you as the teacher. You need to decide how to collect, store, and organize it.

We'll start with behavior data. Since I was the special education teacher, there were times I needed behavior data from a classroom teacher and I could not be in there to collect it personally. I needed the collection to be smooth, easy to understand and do, and quick because I knew how precious time was for all teachers. Something I did to make it simpler was use google forms for data collection. Sometimes I used a numerical scale. For instance, if I was asking how often the student needed to be redirected, it might be very often (10 or more times), often (6-9), occasionally (3-5), minimally (1-2), or not at all (no redirection given). The teachers could pull up the form, mark the corresponding box, and submit it. Using Google forms made it easy for teachers to complete and share with me where it would be saved. There was no having to keep up with various papers.

When it comes to student behavior, you might be counting how many times in one class a student blurts out an answer or gets up from their seat. You might be timing how long it takes a student to open a textbook when first told to do so. That's straight forward data collection. I liked making tally marks to count or putting a time into a table. That's also tied into conducting an observation, but for this type of data, you're watching and collecting data on a specific action, so just keeping track of the total number or marking the time is fine.

When I was collecting behavior data, I had a clicker. When a behavior occurred, I'd click it and it kept track of the total number of clicks. There was my data. I could also just use simple tally marks. Sometimes I used timers, often just using the stopwatch or timer on my phone and noting the duration. It doesn't have to be anything fancy. Amazon has affordable clickers and timers if you're looking for some.

For academic data, I did a few different things. At the beginning of the year, I made each student a binder. Each one had a section for each goal. In the sections, I had my data collection sheets where I'd write scores or percentages and maybe a little snippet of notes like if a student wasn't feeling well that day which could have contributed to a lower score than expected. I also made a bar graph where students could color in the bar for each score and feel a greater sense of ownership over their goals. They loved tracking their own progress. Doing so inspired them to work harder to color each bar graph's score a little higher each time. Also, in each section, I would put the assessments or worksheets I'd be using for progress monitoring. That way, everything I needed was all in one place.

I also had my digital binder that had everything I needed for my whole caseload all in one place: student info, IEP forms, and progress monitoring sheets where I could just input a score to use later for progress reports.

This is a sample of one of the progress monitoring sheets I had in my digital binder. There were four blank boxes under each month for weekly progress monitoring scores. Because it was digital, I would keep the whole thing bookmarked on my desktop and open it as needed to collect student data, enter the data into the table, and have it immediately when it was time for progress reports. This was a very effective method, because it took less time and was conveniently located for easy access instead of having to find a separate folder or binder each time.

Finally, Google sheets is another good option for collecting data. It's just a spreadsheet, but you can do a whole lot of different things with it, such as averages, and tracking multiple students at once.

For larger class sizes, you might prefer the ease and speed of a Google sheet. For my small groups, however, I like taking my notes on paper and then adding scores to my digital notebook. Take your preferences into consideration, and you'll find what works for you.

USING PROGRESS MONITORING DATA TO INFORM DECISIONS

Once you have your answer to these questions and you know what method, frequency, and tools you will use for progress monitoring, it is time to buckle down and dig into the data. One of the easiest ways to see if the instruction and interventions are successful for the student is through the use of a simple, one quadrant graph.

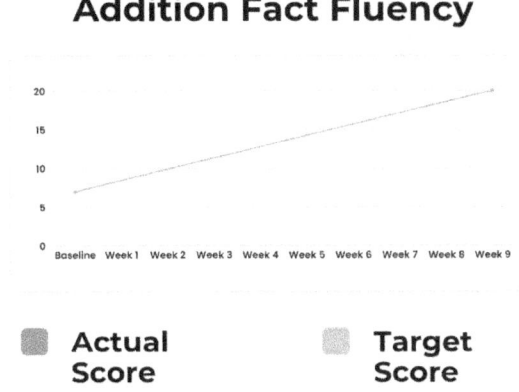

Addition Fact Fluency

In my example, I've plotted scores pertaining to addition fact fluency. On the graph, I first plotted the baseline score and the score my student needed to achieve for mastery—the "goal score." On the graph to the left, you'll see a baseline score of 7 and a goal score of 20. The baseline score is the average score the student received prior to receiving interventions. By connecting the baseline score to the goal score, I was able to graph a line that reflected a probable track for my student's progress.

Beginning on week one, I used this same graph to track progress for each of the 9 weeks in the quarter. Each week as I collected data, I plotted the scores on the same graph and compared the actual scores to the weekly target scores. At the end of that 9 weeks, I would notice one of three things happening.

1. The student's scores would closely follow the target line, showing the interventions and accommodations the student received were sufficient, and the goal was appropriate for them.

Addition Fact Fluency

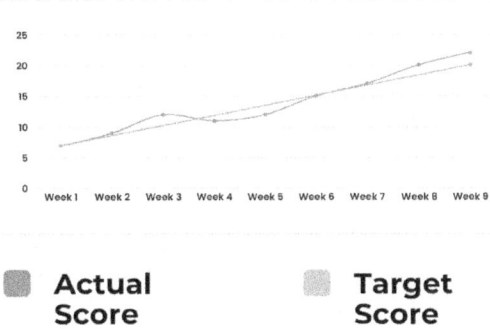

Actual Score **Target Score**

2. The student's scores would fall consistently below the target line, showing the interventions and accommodations were insufficient, and/or the goal was too challenging for them.

Addition Fact Fluency

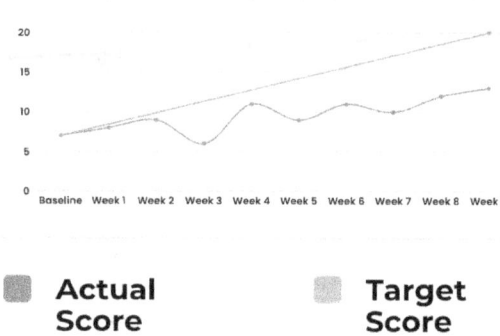

Actual Score   Target Score

3. The student's scores were consistently above the target line, showing the interventions and accommodations might be providing more support than the student needed, and/or the goal was not challenging enough for them.

Addition Fact Fluency

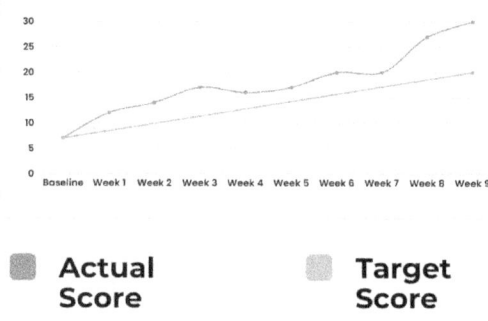

Actual Score   Target Score

You can use these graphs to track data as well. Armed with the graphs, you'll be ready to present data that will drive decision-making when it comes to your students' IEPs. Should goals be increased? Should instructional changes be made? What does your data show? As a member of your student's IEP team, the data you collect throughout the assessment process is vital. But once you've collected it, what do you do with it?

1. IDENTIFY PATTERNS AND TRENDS

As you are collecting your data, you might notice that scores on academic assessments are lower on Mondays than on Fridays. You might notice that particular behavior occurs more frequently before lunch or after PE. Reviewing collected data can reveal patterns and trends showing other how factors might be contributing to a student's success or lack thereof. There are a plethora of internal and external factors that impact a student's ability to make progress. Some children are split between two custodial guardians, living with one or the other every other week. If you begin to see that every other Monday one child's data shows a decline, it could be that they aren't getting enough sleep during the weekend spent with a certain guardian. Noting patterns in the data can help you create a hypothesis as to what some of those factors might be.

> **66** Reviewing collected data can reveal patterns and trends showing others how factors might be contributing to a student's success or lack thereof. **99**

2. ADJUST INSTRUCTIONAL STRATEGIES

Looking at the data can help you determine if adjustments need to be made to instructional strategies being utilized with students. The data will reveal which strategies are working successfully and which may need to be modified.

For example, you might find that one student is more successful when using manipulatives to work through math problems than when manipulatives are not provided, like my student Camilla who thrived when using counting tokens to work through math problems. This data can help justify adding the use of math manipulatives as an accommodation in a student's IEP.

3. MODIFY IEP GOALS AND SERVICES

Progress monitoring data is key to creating and amending IEP goals and special education services portions, as well. By comparing the student's current performance to the established goals outlined in their IEP, educators can determine whether adjustments are necessary. If a student is consistently meeting or exceeding their goals, it may be time to consider raising the bar to ensure continued growth. On the other hand, if progress is slower than expected, goals and services can be revised to provide more targeted support.

When a new student, "Ty," transferred into my fourth-grade class in October 2019, I inherited a new IEP. His goal was being able to read 80% of the fourth-grade level sight words by the end of the year. In my initial reading assessment, I learned that Ty was unable to correctly identify all the letters of the alphabet—a skill considerably lower than his IEP goal. Additionally, he struggled when reading primer level sight words, much less words at his grade level. He needed instruction in letter identification and phonemic awareness. And after waiting a few weeks to see if he would recoup any missing skills, his general education teacher and I felt it necessary to hold a meeting with the rest of the IEP team to rewrite his goals in order to meet him where he was and improve the skills he needed to make progress.

4. COLLABORATE WITH THE IEP TEAM

As you know, the IEP team consists of the special education teacher, the general education teacher, any related service providers, a LEA (Lead Education Agency) Representative, the student, and the student's family/caregivers. Regular communication and sharing progress monitoring data allows all stakeholders to contribute valuable insights and perspectives. Guidelines for sharing progress reports with students' families are even covered in one section of the IEP—outlining how often families will receive information. The IEP can use the data to drive decisions regarding the student's overall school experience. Teachers can offer firsthand observations of the student's progress in the classroom, families can provide insights into the student's performance based on factors outside of school, and related service providers can offer expertise in specific areas of need.

As you can see, progress monitoring goes well beyond collecting grades. It's an essential process that drives every decision made on a student's educational journey. When we decided to amend Ty's IEP goals, that wasn't a decision I made on my own. I relied on input from Ty's general education teacher about skills she saw that he was missing and needed in order to make progress. I sought input from Ty's Occupational Therapist on ways we could provide him with additional support. I talked with Ty's mother about what she was seeing at home and how he performed at his previous school. Our collaborative approach ensured that our decisions were well-rounded and considered the needs of the whole child.

CHAPTER 11:
NAVIGATING CHALLENGES AND OVERCOMING BARRIERS

While we are using our progress monitoring data and collaborating with the other members of the IEP team to look for academic deficiencies that might be playing a role in our students' ability to learn, there is something else that can play a significant factor, as well—their behavior.

When I'm talking to teachers at conferences, it doesn't matter what state I'm in, what grade or subject they teach. Each educator I speak with often has the same question: how can I support positive student behavior in the classroom? We can be doing everything right—creating engaging lessons, boosting student motivation, providing all the necessary accommodations, but student behavior also contributes to a lack of academic progress in the classroom.

> " Just like many students do not come to school knowing how to read and write, some might walk in the door not knowing how to self-regulate. "

Just like many students do not come to school knowing how to read and write, some might walk in the door not knowing how to self-regulate. They might not know how to express their feelings, wants, and needs appropriately. But just like we teach reading, math, and science in our inclusive classrooms, we must be willing to teach these behavioral skills, as well. And that starts with developing specific classroom expectations for accepted behavior that are explicitly taught to students.

ESTABLISHING EXPECTATIONS

Restorative practices occur after an expectation has not been met or an unexpected behavior occurs. So the first step when it comes to restorative practices is simply setting up classroom expectations so students know what behaviors are expected and permitted.

At the beginning of every school year, I shocked my students by informing them that my classroom had *no rules!* That statement was often met with confused looks, maybe some cheers, and always questions: "What do you mean 'no rules?' Does that mean we get to do whatever we want?" And that led to my favorite part—open discussion. I would start by asking the students what a classroom might look like with "no rules."

The answers were usually quite honest:

- It would be loud
- Everybody would be running around
- People might throw stuff
- Kids might get in a fight
- Nobody would get to learn

Then, I would ask them if that sounded like a classroom they really wanted to be in. And while there might be a few jokers in the room, the vast majority said "no."

From there, we would talk about what we wanted our classroom to look and sound like. The whole class discussed which behaviors would be okay, and which we wouldn't want in the classroom. Together, we'd brainstorm a list of characteristics for a "successful" classroom and let those shape our classroom expectations.

To do this exercise, I would use a large piece of anchor chart paper and markers. On the top of the anchor chart paper, I'd write the words "A Successful Classroom…" and beneath that, I'd divide the paper into three zones, labeling each zone: "looks like," "sounds like," "feels like." We would discuss: "What do we want our classroom to look like?" Students would come up with answers like "clean" and "organized." Answers for what we wanted our classroom to sound like might include things like "like we're having fun" or "not super loud."

Once, a student suggested our classroom have soft music playing while the students were working. I was able to use that suggestion as a voice meter: "If you can't hear the music, your voice is too loud!" It was a great way to prompt students to determine if they were being too loud and take responsibility to control their own volume. It greatly reduced the number of times I had to say, "Quiet voices!" and made the whole classroom feel much calmer.

When asked what they wanted our classroom to feel like, 100% of the time, no matter the age or grade of the students I did this exercise with, the students wanted the classroom to feel happy and safe. Other answers included things like "welcoming" and "friendly." This exercise got students to really consider what makes a classroom successful.

The next question I posed was "What do we need to do to make our classroom look, sound, and feel like these things?" From there, it was time to start making our list of expectations.

> **We need to be proactive in addressing behavior rather than reacting to behavior that's already happened.**

I learned very quickly that it's important to develop expectations *with* your students instead of *for* your students. Doing so helps them take ownership of the classroom.

Sharing development of expectations also increases their sense of responsibility and promotes autonomy and self-advocacy. It helps them "buy in" to meeting and abiding by the expectations because they had a say in their creation (just like with the music and volume in my classroom).

Another essential key when developing a list of expectations is to make sure it's stated using positive language. In other words, it's important to focus on what students *will* do instead of what they *won't* do. For example, if one of the expectations is that students won't run in the classroom, that leaves room for loopholes and exemptions. We've all heard children say things like, "I wasn't *running*; I was *skipping!*" They are masters at finding these little loopholes, and you know what? They're right. The rule is, no running.

When you state expectations using positive language, you cut out the margin for loopholes because you are stating what *is* allowed. Instead of "No running in the classroom" the expectation becomes "We walk safely in the classroom to get from location to location." If all we are doing is telling them what NOT to do, how are they supposed to learn what appropriate behavior is? We need to be explicit in this instruction so we are being proactive in addressing behavior rather than reacting to behavior that's already happened.

Once my class had our list of expectations, I would write "In our classroom, we..." and the students would fill in the expectations. The most important part of our list of expectations is that every student and I would sign our names like a classroom contract. I hung our poster on the wall as a visual reminder of the expectations and our responsibility to uphold them.

But what happens when the expectations aren't met? What do we do when problematic behavior occurs?

STRATEGIES FOR ADDRESSING BEHAVIOR ISSUES AND PROMOTING SELF-REGULATION

When you do a Google search for a simple definition of behavior, the first thing that pops up is from Google's Dictionary powered by Oxford Languages. Google's definition of behavior is "the way in which… a person acts in response to a particular situation or stimulus." I like this definition for several reasons.

First, it says behavior is a response. Something happens; someone responds. That's behavior. My stomach growls, so I eat a snack. I exercise, so I get tired. I watch a sad scene in a movie, so I cry. Something happens, and I respond: behavior.

Second, it does not put any connotations on the term or say that behavior is either negative or positive. So often, when we hear the word "behavior," we automatically think about "bad behavior." Even when looking for images based on the word "behavior," many that pop up are images of children yelling or crying or pouting. But behavior, like the definition says, is simply someone's response to their situation or a stimulus.

In addition to being a response to a situation or stimulus, behavior can often be the result of feelings we get based on different events. For instance, if I watch a sad movie, I feel sad, and then I cry. The resulting behavior comes from the feeling I get from a situation. It's the same for our students.

UNDERSTANDING BEHAVIOR AS COMMUNICATION

One of the things I say more than anything else when I'm speaking to schools or conferences is that behavior is simply communication. When a student displays or exhibits a certain behavior, that behavior is communicating a feeling.

Before we go any further, it is essential that I make one thing very clear: all feelings are valid. How a student feels is how they feel, regardless of if you think they're blowing something out of proportion or not. It's not our job to take away what they're feeling. Now, how they express it might need to change, but the feeling itself is real and allowed to exist.

During one of my years as a teacher, I had a student who felt things very strongly. One day she came into school crying her heart out. When I asked what happened to make her so sad, she told me her dog died. I don't know about you, but the death of a pet always gets me right in my feels. I've lost beloved pets before, and I know how impactful that loss can be. As you can imagine, I felt awful for her. She drew pictures of her dog and her family all together, and that made her feel better. Eventually, she calmed down enough and we went about our day.

At pick up that afternoon, I told her mom, "Oh my goodness, your daughter told me about the family dog. I am so sorry!" Her mom looked at me with a very confused expression, and asked me what happened. I explained that her child was very sad that day due to the death of the dog. The mother started to smile a little bit and shook her head. It turned out the dog had died over the summer—*months* before. I joined in the parent's head shake and said, "Well, she was really feeling that loss *today!*"

Does it make sense to you or me (or the student's mom) that months after the dog had passed that the student was so distraught? Not necessarily, but that's not the point. My student was responding to a situation that made her feel sad. Her sadness caused her to exhibit a behavior that was impeding her learning. It needed to be addressed, so we addressed it.

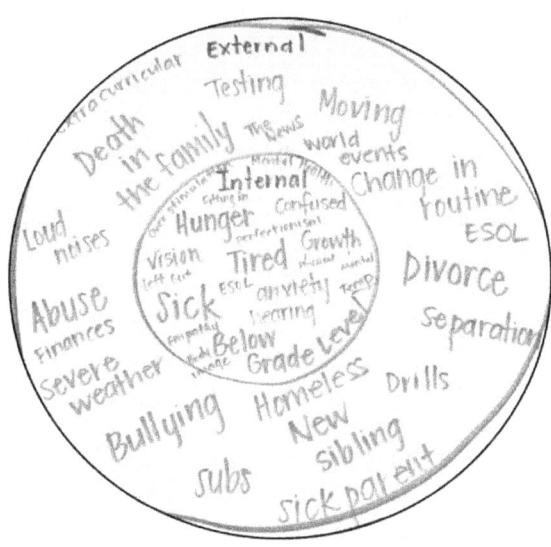

FACTORS THAT CONTRIBUTE TO STUDENT BEHAVIOR

When it comes to factors that contribute to student behavior, some are external, meaning they're things happening to the student. Others are internal, meaning they're things happening within the student.

The image below shows an activity I had teachers do in a professional development session where they brainstormed some of these potential factors. Let's dive into a few examples together.

New Sibling: Having a new baby at home is an exciting time! But it also disrupts everything an older child has considered "normal" in their life. Suddenly, they must share attention with a new sibling. They might be kept awake at night by the baby crying. So while having a new sibling is fun and wonderful, it can also lead to some unpleasant feelings that might impact how a student acts at school. This could look like exhibiting more attention-seeking behavior or falling asleep during class.

Missing a loved one: This could be a family member who lives far away or perhaps someone who passed away. It could even be as simple as missing a parent that dropped them off at school and who will pick them up in a few hours. Regardless of how long it's been, missing someone can contribute to feelings which impact student behavior. They could be much more sensitive, letting things bother them more than usual or they might have bigger reactions to things than they normally would.

Divorce/Custody Changes: This is such a difficult one to navigate. If the child is suddenly going back and forth to different homes with different parents or other guardians, that's a huge change. On top of adjusting to a new normal, each home might be very different. One house might have one set of rules while the other has a different set of expectations. This shift could cause any number of dysregulated emotions and actions. Anger is common; trying to gain a sense of control is common. This is always a delicate situation, and should be handled as such.

All these situations and scenarios can influence student behavior. And typically, you will find that the behavior stems from one of the following feelings. And you can remember the list using the acronym **BATHESSS**: **B**ored, **A**ngry, **T**ired, **H**ungry, **E**nergized, **S**ad, **S**cared, and **S**ick. Note that this is not a comprehensive list, but I have seen that most behavior communicates one of these feelings more often than not:

1. **Bored**: We've all seen those students in our classrooms who are not paying attention. They're flipping pencils, rocking back in chairs, and trying to get other students to talk to them. For whatever reason, they're not engaged in the lesson.

2. **Angry**: Lots of problematic behaviors stem from a place of anger or frustration. It might look like huffing and puffing, fighting, or talking back. Anger is a strong feeling that usually has aggressive or loud behaviors tied to it. It puts the blame for a situation on someone else. Usually, it's easier to feel angry over a situation rather than embarrassed or hurt because it projects a problem onto something else.

3. **Tired**: A lack of sleep is scientifically proven to have a negative impact on student behavior. According to the National Heart, Lung, and Blood Institute, "Children who are sleep deficient might be overly active and have problems paying attention. They also might misbehave, and their school performance can suffer. Sleep-deficient children may feel angry and impulsive, have mood swings, feel sad or depressed, or lack motivation" (https://www.nhlbi.nih.gov).

4. **Hungry**: The term "hangry" exists for a reason. There's also a reason why the Snickers slogan for a while was "You're not you when you're hungry." Being hungry can make you act differently. It can make you react differently. Perhaps you'll have a shorter fuse or be more irritable than usual. I know that's true for me. It's true for our students, as well.

5. **Energized**: Being overly energized or excited can make it difficult to sit still or pay attention to a lesson. Just think about your class on Halloween or Valentine's Day! They're all excited, possibly all sugared up. It can be difficult to keep them engaged in a lesson when you're competing with candy or costumes!

6. **Sad**: There's a whole spectrum to sadness. In an extreme state, it can be depression. Sadness can be caused by something as simple as not being first in line. It's a very broad cause for behavior. But again, it's a valid feeling, even if the reason for it seems minor.

7. **Scared**: We also call it feeling nervous, anxious, or worried. All these ways to say we feel scared can cause a student to shut down or get defensive. It could be something major or something minor. Personally, one of my biggest fears is of the dentist. When I have a dental appointment coming up, it's all I can think about! It can make getting my work done a struggle because I'm so preoccupied by what's to come. If I feel that way as an adult with a fully formed brain, imagine how a ten-year-old might feel!

8. **Sick**: Hopefully if you have a very sick student, they are staying home. But if it's not severe enough, like maybe just a cold or allergies, they could show up in your class and not act like themselves. It's no wonder why. Not feeling well can impede a student's ability to learn and pay attention, and as someone who's been sick before, I can relate.

When a student is engaging in a behavior, it often has nothing to do with you as the teacher and everything to do with them as their own person. The student uses that behavior to communicate their feelings about the situation or stimulus that we talked about earlier.

In our inclusive classrooms, we never try to silence a student. Just like we would never take away a child's communication device if they needed it to talk, we cannot simply remove a behavior that is being used to communicate. Instead, we want to *replace* problematic behaviors with something that serves the same function but is more appropriate for a classroom. So, how do we do that?

DETERMINING THE FUNCTION OF STUDENT BEHAVIOR

The first step to replacing a behavior is determining its function. In the Behavior Analysis world, there are four main categories for the function of behavior: **avoidance**, **access**, **attention**, and **sensory**.

Avoidance Behaviors: A student engaging in avoidance is exhibiting behaviors to get out of doing a task, completing an activity, or escaping a situation they do not want to be in. It might look like the student physically running away. It could also look like the student crumpling up their classwork and throwing it. Perhaps it will look like a student engaging in an off-topic or off-task conversation or activity, such as scrolling through TikTok. Are you wondering how I can come up with so many examples? I've experienced every one of these scenarios at some point in my teaching career.

Access Behaviors: Things that serve this function are exhibited to gain access to a preferred activity, individual, or item. This is the exact opposite of avoidance. It might look like a student racing to be first in line, knocking others out of the way. Or perhaps it looks like a student taking a toy away from another student. It may also look like the student throwing a tantrum when told he can't have something he wants. Access behaviors are often accidentally reinforced when the desired item is given to placate the behavior.

Attention Behaviors: Educators I have talked to cite attention-seeking behaviors as the most problematic ones they encounter in the classroom. It's because any type of attention given can reinforce it. Students engaging in attention-seeking behavior might be considered the "class clown"—attempting to make classmates laugh. It could also look like a student constantly interrupting a lesson. Please note that seeking attention is not inherently a bad thing. We are all social creatures who need attention, connection, and interaction with others. The trouble occurs when it's exhibited in a way that's unsafe, disrupts learning, or is otherwise problematic.

Sensory Behaviors: When this occurs, the behavior itself is reinforcing, meaning the desired outcome is achieved through the action itself. Sensory issues are quite common. A student bouncing their leg while sitting down, tapping a pencil on a desk, or biting their nails are all sensory behaviors. These can become problematic when they disrupt learning, cause harm (or the potential for harm), or when it is a private behavior happening publicly.

Side note: for behaviors that are sensory in nature, I typically let them go unless they are causing harm or are inappropriate for a public setting. If the behaviors are harmful—like a student picking the skin on their fingers or chewing their shirt—providing a chewy or fidget can offer a safer alternative that meets the same sensory need. Even in this instance, the goal is never to be punitive or shameful, as that can further exacerbate symptoms.

When attempting to replace a problematic behavior with a more appropriate one, it is essential to first analyze it and determine which of the four functions it's serving. Remember—the replacement needs to serve the same function. To analyze the behavior, you must first define it by describing what you see. You can't observe someone daydreaming, but you can observe someone staring out of the window, tapping their pencil on the desk, or not completing their assignments. Defining the behavior lets you know exactly what you are replacing and what you are collecting data on.

Once the behavior has been defined, you can start making a hypothesis about its function. To do this, I start at the very beginning with the ABCs of behavior: the antecedent, the behavior, and the consequence. The easiest way to track it is with an ABC Data Sheet.

This is an example of an ABC Data Sheet. At the top, you'll write what behavior the student is exhibiting for which you're trying to determine the function. Be specific; describe it in detail. But only describe what you observe. Remember, it's not personal so keep your own feelings out of it.

In the first column, you will write down the day and time that the behavior occurs. This is very important. You might find that every Tuesday, little Timmy is engaging in the behavior more than usual. You can look at what is happening Tuesdays or even Monday nights and see if there is an overlooked contributing factor. Date and time is very important because it will help you pick up on patterns.

ABCs of student behavior

Describe the behavior

date/ time	antecedent		consequence	
	No Attention Diverted Attention Item Removed	Demand Activity Denied Access	Attention Demand Continued Access to Item	Ignored Demand Removed Removed Item
	No Attention Diverted Attention Item Removed	Demand Activity Denied Access	Attention Demand Continued Access to Item	Ignored Demand Removed Removed Item
	No Attention Diverted Attention Item Removed	Demand Activity Denied Access	Attention Demand Continued Access to Item	Ignored Demand Removed Removed Item
	No Attention Diverted Attention Item Removed	Demand Activity Denied Access	Attention Demand Continued Access to Item	Ignored Demand Removed Removed Item
	No Attention Diverted Attention Item Removed	Demand Activity Denied Access	Attention Demand Continued Access to Item	Ignored Demand Removed Removed Item

@RebekahPoeTeaching

Next, briefly describe the antecedent. This is the A of our ABCs. The antecedent is the event that occurs immediately prior to the behavior. Was the student working with a peer or on his own? Had he just come in from recess? Was he told to open his math binder? Whatever happened immediately before the behavior, note that.

Then, circle the category that encompasses the antecedent. Was Timmy trying to avoid something, trying to get attention, or perhaps having sensory issues?

Once the behavior occurs (the B in our ABCs), you'll also need to note what happens immediately after. This is the consequence, the occurrence that happened due to the student exhibiting the problematic behavior that now needs to be replaced. Did Timmy gain access to what he was wanting or get out of doing something he didn't want to do? Did the teacher go over to where he was? What was the result of the behavior? Write it down, then circle the outcome.

Pretty soon, after a few behavior displays, you'll start noticing a pattern emerge from what you circled for the antecedents and the consequences. Tally up how many were part of which category and that will help you develop a hypothesis of the function. Before you know it, you'll get an idea of whether it was for attention, avoidance, or access, and that will help formulate a replacement behavior.

The replacement needs to serve the same function as the behavior being replaced. If a student is trying to avoid doing something he doesn't want to do, the goal of the replacement behavior isn't to make the child a willing participant. Rather, the goal is to teach the student how to communicate that he is struggling with his assignment in a more appropriate way.

Instead of Timmy shredding the math worksheet because he doesn't want to do it (and ultimately because he doesn't understand it), we want to teach him to either request a break or ask for help. Let's look at each of the functions to determine some strategies and interventions for each.

BEHAVIOR STRATEGIES AND INTERVENTIONS BY FUNCTION

Avoidance

Strategies for avoidance behaviors can vary based on whether or not a situation or stimulus is actually avoidable. Some activities can be avoided, and you want to teach your students how to express their desire not to do something with more acceptable behavior. Tell them that it's okay to say "No, thank you" or "I'd rather not do that right now." Some students don't realize that they have that as an option if they haven't been given the opportunity to be autonomous before, especially if they've been relying on negative behaviors to express their wants and needs.

However, some activities cannot be avoided, like doing classwork. Instead of Timmy throwing away his paper or trying to leave the room, teach him how to ask appropriately for a break. And utilize what he does like.

Remember my student Marcus and his love of toy cars? He was much more willing to do a less preferred activity when a more preferred activity was incorporated and dependent upon the completion of the task. A student interest inventory will show you things a student might be willing to work for. A highly motivating reinforcement (like cars) can be enough to get through the less-preferred activity. We call that the Premack principle—a theory of reinforcement that states that a less desired behavior can be reinforced by the opportunity to engage in a more desired behavior. You can also use a token board to help the student track how many tasks they've done and still have to do to get to that preferred activity or item.

Interventions for Avoidance	
You Got It, Dude	As much as possible, allow an unwanted activity to be avoided when the student exhibits an appropriate behavior to avoid it (for example, calmly saying "No" or "I don't want to" is a better choice than exhibiting the problematic behavior). Especially in the beginning, this will reinforce the positive option of using calm words to express wants and needs.
We Were On a Break	Teach the student to request a break either verbally, with a hand signal, or with a break request card. Practice in safe scenarios before engaging in a triggering task or event. Keep the breaks structured with a time limit. Consider a "one minute warning" to help the student transition from the break back to the activity.
You Earned It	Positively reinforce task completion with a reward of the student's choosing. Use a student interest inventory to determine how the student is motivated to plan rewards.
Countdown	Predetermine a number of tasks for a student to complete. At the end of each, let the student earn one token. Once all tokens are earned, let them exchange the tokens for a reward or break.
First/Then	Sequence a preferred activity after a less-preferred activity. For example, let them know you're doing five math problems, and that afterward, they can have Play-Doh. You can use a written or picture schedule to promote understanding.

Access

For access, the strategies are actually quite similar to those used for avoidance, but in this case, you KNOW what the student prefers and you can use that as your motivating tool to encourage task completion or other positive, expected behaviors. If/then statements are great for this. We might tell a student, "If you finish your spelling list, then you will be able to draw with your new markers." It can work the same way for other things: "If you finish your math lesson, then you can play on the computer for ten minutes." Use what the student wants to gain access to as the reinforcer, and stick with what you said. It will fall apart if the student realizes that he'll still get the reward even if he doesn't meet the requirements.

But what happens if what is desired isn't possible? For example, a student might want to gain access to a snack, when it isn't snack time. Or perhaps they want to stay in the gym playing when it is time to go back to class. Again, showing a written or picture schedule might help the student understand that what he wants will happen later or that the activity is "all done."

Interventions for Access	
You Choose	Allow the student to decide between two choices to complete a task. For example, you could let the student pick a colorful pen to complete work instead of a pencil, or you could allow them to pick between starting with one task or another. Offering choice increases feelings of control and lets the student maintain some autonomy.
Contingency Plan	Allow the student to select a preferred item or activity from a choice board. Explain that participation in the activity or using the fun item is contingent upon completing the less desired task. Let them track task completion using a token board.
X Marks the Spot	Use a behavior chart to track tasks completed or positive behaviors exhibited by putting an X or a sticker on the box for each. When the chart is full, it can be traded in for the desired object or activity.

The Opposite of Avoidance	When you know what the student wants, use that to reinforce appropriate behavior in the classroom. Allow them access to the item when it is requested appropriately.
If/Then	Use If/Then statements to explain consequences. "If you hit a friend, then you will not be able to sit by him." "If you complete this activity, then you can have free time." This helps students learn the correlation between their behavior and the outcome.

Attention

Students will often engage in attention-seeking behavior to establish a connection to the people around them. The goal is to teach the student that they can gain attention when they are on task or participating correctly instead of participating in negative behaviors which demand it. The trick is that often any attention—either positive or negative—can be reinforcing. When attempting to teach a replacement, you must first spend time negating the problematic behavior by removing attention from it. And often, it gets worse before it gets better. But stick with it, because it will get better.

Interventions for Attention	
Star Student	Call out a student who is exhibiting the desired behavior. When the target student follows suit, provide positive attention. This is also called "positive narration."
Play Calling	With your student, develop a set of hand signals you can use to provide attention/redirection as needed. A simple thumbs up can let them know they're on the right track.
Praise, Praise, Praise	If your student is seeking attention, make sure you are providing it for all the right reasons. Especially at first, praise every instance of positive behavior. Make it a big deal!

Now Hiring	Assign a classroom job or role for a student seeking attention. It should be something that naturally generates positive attention in a healthy way, such as being a classroom greeter or teacher's helper.
Withdraw	If a student is used to exhibiting a certain negative behavior to get attention, cut off the supply. As much as you can, do not provide any attention to the negative behavior (if safety allows). This strategy should always be paired with **Praise, Praise, Praise.**

So now comes the question of when and how you teach each strategy. You must be intentional about it. You can't just present a tactic once and expect students to know how to use them.

There are a few ways to teach these skills regularly. Roleplaying is a good exercise in instruction. Come up with scenarios and ask children to tell you the steps they need to take. Modeling appropriate and expected behavior is likewise fantastic. Students can see you modeling the desired behavior and observe what it looks like. This might be a time when something happens that might make you irritated. Model the appropriate way to be frustrated. Narrate your process. It might look something like, "Oh, no! I am out of water in my water bottle, and I'm still thirsty. I can't go to the water fountain right now to refill it; I'll be patient until I have the chance to get more water."

Any teachable moment you get can be used to work on these replacement behaviors. There are a million ways your students could act up but, but guess what? That means there are a million ways to help them. Don't forget: Every intervention should be specific to each child and what their needs are. But never fear. After all, who knows what they need at school better than you?

CHAPTER 12:
DE-ESCALATING STUDENTS IN CRISIS

Teaching comes during teachable moments. But what happens when the student is not teachable, when the problematic behavior becomes too much? This is what I refer to as a "Crisis Moment."

According to the Oxford Languages Dictionary in Google, a crisis is "a time of intense difficulty, trouble, or danger." In such a moment, when a child is feeling extreme stress, the area of the brain that controls "flight, fight, or freeze" takes over, essentially "shutting off" the area of the brain where learning takes place.

Crisis mode can look different based on your student, based on the feelings they have, and based on the behaviors they're exhibiting. There is no one way to know that a student is in crisis.

> **The way we respond to students in crisis can make or break the moment.**

Of course, sometimes it will be obvious. A student who is flipping a table is obviously in crisis. A student crying uncontrollably—obviously in crisis. However, the student who is sitting silently but not doing an assignment you just handed out...that could also be a crisis moment—a moment of intense difficulty.

This is not the time to try to teach. Rather, it's the time to respond. And the way we respond to students in crisis can make or break the moment.

Early in my teaching career, I came across this quote from psychologist and educator Haim Ginott:

> "I've come to a frightening conclusion that I am the decisive element in the classroom. It's my personal approach that creates the climate. It's my daily mood that makes the weather. As a teacher, I possess a tremendous power to make a child's life miserable or joyous. I can be a tool of torture or an instrument of inspiration. I can humiliate or heal. In all situations, it is

my response that decides whether a crisis will be escalated or de-escalated and a child humanized or dehumanized."

Pay attention to that last line especially: "It is my response that decides whether a crisis will be escalated or de-escalated."

I like to use the analogy of comparing a crisis to a fire. If the fire is there, it is happening; it is burning, and what happens next is entirely dependent on what the fire encounters. If fuel is added, the fire continues to grow. It gets bigger and worse until it is all-consuming and almost impossible to stop. On the other hand, if water is added or oxygen is removed, the fire gets smaller and smaller until it goes out or at least gets small enough to handle safely. So if the student's crisis is the fire, what is the teacher's response? Is it fuel or water? How do we respond?

It is human nature to respond to negative behavior in a negative way. That student who is talking back? Of course you want to yell back and place your own demands. It can be so easy to engage in a power struggle with such students. After all, you are the teacher. They are the child and they are "supposed to do what you say."

But as we all have encountered, that's not the way it works. And placing demands or yelling or making threats does nothing but escalate the situation. Worse than that, it completely derails your relationship with them.

Instead, the first thing we have to do is remove our own emotions from the situation and remember that a student's behavior is not personal. I know this is incredibly difficult at times, because I've been through it, too, but remember: we are the crucial elements.

There's a phrase that gets shared online from time to time. It says, "The student is not giving me a hard time; the student is having a hard time." And when we start looking at a child's behavior with that frame, we can better de-escalate the situation.

Q.T.I.P.
Quit Taking It Personally

When I present on this topic, I show the teachers I'm speaking to an image of a Q-Tip on the screen with the words "Quit Taking It Personally" (Q.T.I.P.).

I tell them, just like I'm telling you, that putting a Q-Tip on your desk is a great visual reminder that when things get hard, remember that it's not personal. Even if it feels like it is. Trust me, I've been there. But an escalated adult will never de-escalate a student. It's not possible. It's just gasoline on a fire.

Next time, before responding, take a deep breath. Count to ten. If you need to walk away for a minute to regain your composure, do that. Make sure you are regulated so that you can help the student regulate their emotions, too.

What this does is help you establish yourself as a trustworthy person, someone the student knows is safe who isn't going to leave when things get hard. Some of our students have had plenty of those experiences in their lives, and we don't want to create more.

> **We cannot establish ourselves as constants in our students' lives if we are constantly changing the way we respond to them.**

You've heard that relationships must come first in teaching, and it's true. If relationships are that important for teaching academics, they are even more important when it comes to teaching behavior.

The second thing we must do is stay consistent. We cannot establish ourselves as constants in our students' lives if we are constantly changing the way we respond to them. We need to have consistent expectations and consequences for what happens when those expectations are not met or are exceeded. They need to be as consistent as possible for each student, as well. If it's a rule for one student, it needs to be the same across the board.

But sometimes, even when we keep our cool and provide consistency, our students can still elevate a situation into a full "crisis moment." When a child in our class becomes dysregulated, our first plan of action should always be de-escalation. We can do that by taking a DIVE into the situation at hand.

I use the acronym DIVER to remember the steps to helping students work through crisis moments:

>**D**: Describe what you see
>**I**: Inquire about a feeling
>**V**: Verify the details and Validate the feeling
>**E**: Explore solutions
>**R**: Restore

Through these steps, you will be able to see a resolution to the crisis moment and restore order to a student's chaos, helping things get back on track so you can get back to teaching and the students can get back to learning.

DESCRIBE WHAT YOU SEE

The first step to de-escalation is to describe what you see. Begin by observing the child in crisis and noting exactly what it looks like. Are they crying or yelling?

Is their head down on the desk? What observable behavior are they exhibiting? Stick to what you see and hear. Keep your personal feelings out of it. And be as specific as possible.

Remember my student Carrie whose goal was to choose a non-violent solution during conflict? To make progress on her goal, she first had to be able to identify how she typically responded to stressful situations. She had a very specific "tell" that gave away when she was on the verge of totally losing her cool. Carrie's nostrils would start to flare, her breathing would become heavy, and her eyes would narrow. When I saw that, I knew what was coming.

You'll need to begin by talking to your student and describing the behavior you see. Sometimes in a crisis event, that "fight, flight, or freeze" area of the brain takes over and students react without thinking. Bringing awareness to the behavior, like Carrie's heavier breathing, helps students get their mind back in the present moment.

This is why you need to be specific in your descriptions. You won't tell the student, "I see you're throwing a fit." Instead, you'll describe the actions the student is showing: "I see you're crying and you've thrown your pencil and paper on the ground." This lets the student know you see them and you're in the moment together.

INQUIRE ABOUT A FEELING

Next, you'll need to pair that observable behavior with a suspected feeling to help them recognize how they feel. This is an important piece of teaching a student emotional regulation. If they don't recognize the association between the feeling and the behavior, then their behavior will be ruled by their emotions.

However, it is not only behavior that is affected by a lack of self-regulation skills. According to Graziano, et. al. "These observed deficits in behavioral control negatively impact the student's ability to attend to information presented by teachers as well as complete school related tasks or assignments that foster learning" (2007). For the students in your classroom who already struggle academically due to learning or other disabilities, learning to self-regulate is essential for them to have the best chance for academic success within the general education classroom.

So you might say to the student, "Hey, your nostrils are flaring and you're breathing kind of hard. Are you angry right now?" If the answer is no, ask if they can name the emotion connected to their behavior. There are two things that can happen at this point. They'll either tell you, "I'm feeling this way" or they'll say, "I don't know."

With our students with disabilities, they really might not be able to identify or explain their emotions or feelings. Being able to do so requires significant expressive communication skills. Many children with IEPs struggle with that in one way or another. In this case, you're going to attempt to help them identify a feeling based on what you observed.

You might say, "I think you might be feeling angry, because sometimes when people are breathing hard and their eyes get narrow, it's because they're mad." In that moment, you'll help the student learn to recognize that their behavior is a reaction to an emotion. They'll also learn what that emotion *feels like* in their body.

VERIFY THE DETAILS AND VALIDATE THE FEELING

The next step in the de-escalation process is to verify the details surrounding the situation. You'll want to get the "who, what, where, and when" of what happened.

Notice that I'm not going to ask them "why" something happened. When you ask "why," you just mean: Why did something happen? But for a student, that question can come off as accusatory. They'll go on the defense if they think that you're on the offense. It naturally triggers defense mechanisms. For students who are already triggered and escalated, there is nowhere to go but to continue that downward spiral.

Asking "why" also provides the student with the opportunity to make an excuse for their behavior. When the question is "Why?" the answer usually begins with "Because…" which allows students to place blame onto someone else. So stick with the who, what, when, and where of a situation to get just the facts.

Getting these details is important for several reasons. First of all, you need all the information in order to document the event in case you need to write up a report. The second reason is to be able to document it on your ABC data sheet as the antecedent to the behavior. Finally, and possibly most importantly, it's so you can let the student know that you hear them. Especially when you pair it with the second part of the V, which is "validate the feeling."

Remember that when you are working with a student in crisis, the feeling that leads to the behavior is always valid, even if you don't understand it. Remember my example about my student crying over her dog? If I had said, "That's no reason to cry! Come on, be a big girl!" I would have made the situation worse and damaged my relationship with the student. I might have even caused her to feel like she should repress her feelings or that feeling "sad" is something that is wrong or not allowed.

So once you get the details, it's important to validate that feeling. Repeat the details back to the student so they know you heard them and then keep it simple: "I can see how that would make you feel [tired, angry, frustrated, etc.]." Doing this reaffirms you as someone the student can trust.

EXPLORE SOLUTIONS

When it comes to helping a student find a solution to their crisis, I am going to tell you to do something that goes against the very nature of a teacher. I'm actually going to tell you not to help.

I see you gasping and the wheels spinning in your head. "How can I help if I don't *help?*" The answer is by letting the students explore and suggest solutions themselves. Instead of asking "What can I do to help?" or "What can we do to help you calm down?", try asking, "What can *you* do to feel better right now?" This is crucial, because if the student and I are coming up with a solution together, or if I am doing the calming, what happens next time it occurs and I'm not there?

Remember the goal is *self*-regulation. Put the responsibility of regulating emotions back on the student so the next time it happens, they can recall what they did last time. That's when they can regulate themselves and do it again.

This is why you'll ask your student, "What can you do to feel less [angry, frustrated, etc.] right now?" Then you'll encourage them to come up with a solution on their own that they can regain control of their own emotions. It might be that the student needs to take a small break away from their work or go get a drink from the water fountain. If it is a feasible solution, allow it. And then check back in with the student upon their return.

What if the solution the student suggests is something that is not feasible or not allowed? For example, let's say you have someone who is steaming mad at a peer. Let's say you ask, "What can you do to feel less angry right now?" and the student replies with "I can punch him in his face; that would make me feel better." While that might be the case, it's certainly not allowed. It's not a feasible solution. In that instance, you can ask for another suggestion or you make a suggestion yourself. But the key is allowing the student to follow through with the solution in order to regain composure and regulate themselves emotionally.

RESTORE

After a solution has been established and the crisis has been de-escalated, you will want to follow up with the student. This is where the teachable moment is possible, because the student is finally out of that "fight or flight" mode and has regained control of their emotions. Take this time to talk through what happened.

For example, you might say, "You were really angry. You yelled at your friends and threw your paper on the ground. How do you feel after taking a break and getting some water? What can you do the next time you start to feel so angry?"

By reinforcing the solution you're reinforcing the student's use of their own self-regulation skills. The goal is that, hopefully, the next time something happens which would typically lead to a crisis moment, your student can remember what solution was the best option.

This is not something that is going to be a "one and done" situation. Remember, I was collecting data for Carrie's behavior goal over months. The goal wouldn't be considered mastered until she was able to safely respond to conflict every time over the course of a nine-week period! As with all our academic instruction, education in the area of behavior and self-regulation takes repeated opportunities to practice. But by "diving" into your student's crisis, you will be able to meet them where they are and work from there.

Remember, it takes time to learn something and even longer for it to become a habit. Fortunately, what you've done by taking time to effectively communicate through the crisis is help the student calm down and control themselves. You've let the student know that they're safe and understood. Crucially, you've also added another layer to that vital teacher/student relationship.

ADDRESSING THE AFTERMATH

When the crisis is over, the behavior has stopped, and the student is regulated. However, problematic behavior occurred that must be dealt with. We cannot allow students to shirk responsibility or place blame on someone else for their actions. The regulation occurs so that restoration can also occur. This takes place through the use and implementation of consequences and restorative practices.

> **The regulation occurs so that restoration can also occur.**

PUNISHMENTS VERSUS CONSEQUENCES

Before going further, it is important to address the difference between punishments and consequences. Often the terms are used interchangeably, but they mean very different things. Merriam Webster defines "punishment" as "suffering, pain, or loss that serves as retribution; a penalty inflicted on an offender; severe, rough, or disastrous treatment." The definition of "consequence" is "a conclusion derived through logic; something produced by a cause or necessarily following from a set of conditions." Punishment is something done to someone based their actions. Consequences are things that happen due to someone's actions.

Consequences can be categorized as natural or logical (sometimes referred to as imposed consequences). Natural consequences are the consequences that occur, you guessed it, naturally based on a prior action. An example could be a child leaving her Barbie doll on the floor instead of putting it away and the child's pet dog using it as a chew toy and amputating both of the doll's hands (this may or may not have been an occurrence at my house a few years ago). Because the child didn't put her doll away (even after her mother reminded her one million times), the dog found it overnight and chewed it up. That is a natural consequence of her action.

Logical or imposed consequences occur as the reasonable result of an action and directly relate to the action itself. They also typically require the righting of a wrong. An example of a logical consequence could be a child playing inappropriately with a friend's toy and breaking it. His parents may have him apologize and complete chores around the house to earn money to replace it. In both cases, whether the consequences are natural or logical, they teach accountability for actions and behavior. Consequences are a learning tool that can be used to reinforce appropriate choices and behaviors.

Punishments, however, are often less specific to the action or behavior. The danger that comes from prioritizing punishment over consequences is that it focuses more on controlling problematic behavior rather than reinforcing positive behavior. It typically comes from a place of emotional reaction and leads to a greater emotional reaction from the student, often based in fear or shame. Additionally, punishments do not teach students to take responsibility for their actions, nor do they teach them to problem-solve alternative, more appropriate solutions to the situation that contributed to their negative behavior.

An example of a punishment that I have seen repeatedly is a student getting in trouble and losing recess privileges for anything in the classroom. Let's say a student fought with a friend, and as a punishment, they are each made to sit out at recess. So they sit on the sidewalk, angry—at their friend for fighting and at their teacher for making them sit out. As far as that instance goes, yes—the behavior stopped. But the situation hasn't been resolved. No instruction occurred to help the children choose better alternatives the next time emotions rise.

Please note that I am not saying a student shouldn't get in trouble when he has done something wrong. What I am saying however, is that the trouble should be a logical consequence of the action and not based on our emotion. Remember, we shouldn't take our students' behavior personally, nor should we base consequences off our feelings about the behavior.

Losing recess alone isn't necessarily a logical consequence because it is not addressing the complexity of the behavior. When imposing logical consequences, there are three things to consider:

1. Logical consequences should directly relate to the action/behavior displayed.

2. Logical consequences work best to reinforce behavior when they are implemented swiftly and consistently.

3. Logical consequences should provide an opportunity for discussion of the behavior and instruction on better choices that could be made in the future.

Those three qualities ensure that students aren't simply being punished for bad behavior, but that they are working to restore order, as well as the relationship or environment.

DISPROPORTIONALITY IN SCHOOL DISCIPLINE

According to recent studies, students with disabilities, especially those impacting social-emotional skills and behavior, are up to four times more likely to receive exclusionary punishments such as suspension or expulsion as their non-disabled peers. A school in Rhode Island was found to have 13% of its student body receiving special education services. However, those students made up 30% of suspensions related to disorderly conduct and 21% of suspensions for insubordination. Unfortunately, those findings seem to be the norm across the nation.

For students with disabilities, who may already be behind their typical peers in academic and behavioral skills, the lack of instruction and services during a suspension only serves to deepen the disparities. It's because exclusionary practices don't get to the root of the problem. They don't teach alternative behaviors for problem solving. They are a reactive approach to punishing problematic behavior, and they don't work.

Instead, students need to learn self-regulation strategies and problem-solving techniques. They need to learn replacement behaviors that serve the same function as the problematic issues they currently exhibit. And this needs to occur from the start. Addressing behavior proactively can help reduce the instances of problematic behaviors that lead to exclusionary punishment. So how do we do that?

RESTORATIVE PRACTICES

Restoration is an essential ending to a crisis moment. It can look like restoring the classroom environment, restoring relationships between students and teachers, or restoring relationships between peers.

A practice that is becoming more and more common in schools and classrooms is the idea of restorative justice. It's "a broad term that encompasses a growing social movement to institutionalize non-punitive, relationship-centered approaches for avoiding and addressing harm, responding to violations of legal and human rights, and collaboratively solving problems" (Fronius, et al, 2019). In the school system, restorative justice focuses on nurturing and repairing relationships rather than managing behavior. It is viewed as a proactive response to problematic student behavior. Importantly, the goal is reducing exclusionary punishments such as suspension or expulsion which, as we discussed, have been shown to do more harm than good.

In a 2021 study conducted by the American Institute for Research for New York public schools, researchers found that "disciplining students through suspensions and expulsions did not reduce future misbehavior for the disciplined students or their peers. It also did not generate improved academic achievement or perceptions of positive school climate" (NEA Today). In fact, the study further discovered a correlation between the severity of the punishment and the negative impact on the punished student's attendance, academic success, and overall feelings regarding the school.

I have certainly seen this among students, particularly in secondary grades. They get in trouble; they get suspended; they come back angry and resentful. It can take a while to build back the relationship you had with a student after all of that.

Restorative justice allows students the opportunity to take accountability and accept the natural and/or logical consequences of their actions while supporting the emotional and social development of the child. When implemented with fidelity, restorative practices not only decrease problematic student behavior and exclusionary punishment, but they also improve the culture and climate of the school. It positively influences the feelings of students, faculty, and staff. But where and how do we start?

Just like it's important to have your students participate in the creation of classroom expectations, it is also important to have students participate in repairing the harm caused when those expectations aren't met.

In the book *Hacking School Discipline*, authors Nathan Maynard and Brad Weinstein write:

> "Conflicts are opportunities for students to understand the impact of their behavior, understand their obligation to take responsibility for their actions, and take steps toward making things right. Allowing them to work through the problem and develop their own ways to repair the harm sets the foundation to change their behaviors permanently, rather than just putting a Band-Aid on a single situation" (p. 65).

Furthermore, restorative practices allow for a structured, consistent stage for students to do just that, particularly the practice of classroom circles.

Classroom circles function as both a preventative behavioral strategy and a strategy that can be used after a behavior occurs during a conflict. The goal of a classroom circle may be to check in with students and get a meter on their emotional well-being. It can also be to address tension in relationships when trust has been broken. But most importantly, classroom circles promote two important goals of restorative practices. The first is building community. The second is responding to unmet expectations or conflicts through effective communication.

While the actual practice of restorative classroom circles might vary depending on the specifics of the situation, the overall framework of it is largely the same. The University of San Diego offers five steps for outlining their structure:

1. All involved parties discuss the incident in question.

2. The victim will be given the opportunity to share their feelings, as will the accused. Restorative practices must provide equal time to each party as the primary goal is not punishment, but restoration.

3. Teachers/administrators will act as facilitators to the mediation, where they ask open-ended questions to foster reflection. These group meetings are known as circles and are central to restorative justice practices.

4. Questions posed to students often include: What can you do to fix this? How would you feel if the same thing happened to you? How did your behavior impact your fellow students?

5. All involved parties decide on a course of action, and all parties work together to carry out that plan.

To start implementing your classroom circles tomorrow, there are several steps you should take. You'll want to start by establishing expectations for the circle. The circle needs to be a safe space where judgements and assumptions are not allowed. A "facts only" rule for communication will help keep that expectation, along with using a "talking piece." This is always something tangible and usually large enough to be visible to others that one student can hold in their hands when it's their turn to speak.

In the past, I've had success using a stuffed animal as the talking piece. My students found it comforting as they held it, and they typically took great care when passing it to one another. Regardless of what you choose to use, make sure that only the person holding the talking piece is allowed to talk.

To promote effective communication, encourage the use of "I" statements that focus on the speaker's thoughts, feelings, and experiences. As the teacher, you can also model empathetic listening. You'll want to repeat back that you hear how the student is feeling and that you validate their feeling, just like we did in our de-escalation strategy. Encourage other students to do the same. From there, decide on the action plan to repair the harm caused by the problematic behavior. Does the student need to apologize to anyone or clean up an area? Do privileges need to be revoked until there is trust earned back?

Once the environment is restored, return to class as usual. You may choose a quiet independent activity to have your students complete (like silent reading) if they need some time to decompress. If logical consequences need to be imposed on any one student or group of students, do that separately so as not to bring shame to or labeling of the student(s) by their peers.

I know that this seems like a lot of time and effort to put in on top of teaching an already full load of academics and having to battle the clock to make sure everything fits into your class time. But consider the difference you can make by taking a small amount of time for restorative circles perhaps a couple of times a week at the beginning of the year. Now consider the converse. If you don't take time to set the stage for restorative circles, you'll constantly be redirecting and correcting student behavior multiple times a day or even multiple times an hour. Do you want to do that all year long again? I certainly don't. It's easy to see that the time spent proactively responding to behavior cuts down on the number of times problematic behavior is exhibited.

Remember that the goal is to reduce the behavior through strategies such as de-escalation techniques and restorative practices by teaching self-regulation and social/emotional skills. In turn, this will lessen the reliance of the exclusionary punishments that plague our most at-risk students.

Picture walking into a classroom where each student is engaged, not because you are constantly directing them, but because they've learned to regulate their emotions and take responsibility for their own learning. This is my goal as a teacher. The atmosphere should be less about managing behavior and more about guiding and supporting, allowing you to spend more time teaching your students than reacting to them. Knowing you've created a space where learning thrives and each student feels a sense of belonging is a victory. And now you know the steps to take to make this dream a reality!

CONCLUSION

Inclusive education is not just about meeting legal requirements; it's about fostering an environment where all students can thrive. But it's also about making sure you as the educator have the skills and tools you need to meet each student where they are. From initial eligibility and implementing IEPs to helping students learn essential skills, it is imperative that you know how each process works and what your role is in each of them.

But knowing the strategies and being able to implement them are only part of the fabric of inclusive education. A key factor of whether inclusive education will be successful or not is teacher buy-in. If teachers are fully committed, it works!

Earlier I quoted Haim Ginott when he said, "I am the decisive element in the classroom." He was right. However, it can be difficult to buy into something (much less implement it) if you don't know enough about it.

> **When students are included in the classroom in a way that they truly feel they belong and are seen, heard, understood, and validated, there are massive changes.**

Since inclusion is a mindset, and I'm the decisive element in my room, then it's my mindset that brings the inclusion. You have that power too. It's a decision you make and a belief you hold that every student in your classroom has a place and a purpose in being there. It's an attitude of breaking the stigma and the cycle associated with special education and IEPs. It's about ensuring that students are not simply sitting in your classrooms, but that they are valued, welcome members of your classroom community.

To provide inclusive education successfully, teachers must embrace the mindset that every student can and should be fully included—not just merely present. A positive attitude toward inclusion is one of the earliest indicators of a successful program. Being willing to work as a team, with general and special education teachers, service providers, and families, is what's necessary to give students the best chance at success.

But it's not just academics that see benefits from inclusive education. When students are included in the classroom in a way that they truly feel they belong and are seen, heard, understood, and validated, there are massive changes. That's when we see improvements in overall classroom behavior, decreases in exclusionary punishments, and a better overall attitude towards school as a whole.

For me, it's made a world of a difference. I have seen students who started the year angry at the world with a chip on their shoulders discover that they have a place to belong. I've seen classes come together to achieve goals greater than anyone thought possible. I've seen friendships formed and relationships built. And I know that the outcomes are not based on any one specific thing I've done, but by embracing a mindset of inclusion and truly believing that every single student who enters my classroom deserves to be there.

Diane Richler, past president of Inclusion International, says "Inclusion is not a strategy to help people fit into the systems and structures which exist in our societies; it is about transforming those systems and structures to make it better for everyone."

You have the power to make a truly inclusive classroom. And it all starts today.

ABOUT THE AUTHOR

Rebekah Poe is an award-winning special education teacher and a national teaching conference presenter with over a decade of experience in the special education field. As an education consultant, Rebekah's passion is providing teachers with the training necessary to offer equitable education and establish connections to students of all ability levels in an inclusive setting. When she's not in the classroom, she can be found at the closest coffee shop with a piping hot latte and a good book. She lives in Alabama with her husband Andrew,  daughter Parker, and their pets—two cats, a dog, and an axolotl.

Stay Connected: Join the conversation and keep up-to-date with Rebekah Poe on social media:

Instagram: @rebekahpoeteaching
Facebook: @rebekahpoeteaching

Inquiries and Contact: For any questions or more information, feel free to reach out to Rebekah directly at hello@rebekahpoeteaching.com. She's eager to connect with fellow educators and share ideas for creating inclusive learning environments.

MORE FROM
BLUEPRINT FOR INCLUSION

Ready to dive deeper into the ideas and strategies shared in *Blueprint for Inclusion*? Rebekah Poe offers a wealth of resources, professional development opportunities, and ways to stay connected with a community of passionate educators dedicated to inclusive teaching practices.

- **Professional Development**: Visit www.rebekahpoeteaching.com for more information about personalized, book-based professional development sessions. Rebekah offers workshops, webinars, and training designed to help educators implement the strategies in *Blueprint for Inclusion* and create truly inclusive classrooms. Whether you're seeking group sessions for your school or district or individual coaching, Rebekah's guidance can help you bring the book's principles to life.

- **Teaching Resources**: Explore a wide range of teaching resources that complement the ideas presented in *Blueprint for Inclusion* https://rebekahpoeteaching.com/shop/ From lesson plans and classroom tools to inclusive teaching materials, these resources are designed to make implementing inclusion practices simple and effective.

Let's work together to make every classroom a place where all students can succeed!

REFERENCES

Centers for Disease Control and Prevention. (n.d.). Autism spectrum disorder (ASD). Retrieved from https://www.cdc.gov/ncbddd/autism/index.html

ERIC. (2016). Universal design for learning and differentiation strategies. Retrieved from https://files.eric.ed.gov/fulltext/EJ1118529.pdf

Frontiers in Education. (2019). Co-teaching strategies for inclusive classrooms. Retrieved from https://www.frontiersin.org/journals/education/articles/10.3389/feduc.2019.00081/full

IRIS Center, Peabody Vanderbilt University. (n.d.). Accommodations and modifications in the classroom. Retrieved from https://iris.peabody.vanderbilt.edu/module/acc/cresource/q2/p04/

Medical News Today. (2019). Assistive technology for students with disabilities. Retrieved from https://www.medicalnewstoday.com/articles/325106

National Center for Education Statistics. (2023). Students with disabilities. Retrieved from https://nces.ed.gov/programs/coe/indicator/cgg/students-with-disabilities

Pew Research Center. (2023). What federal education data shows about students with disabilities in the U.S. Retrieved from https://www.pewresearch.org/short-reads/2023/07/24/what-federal-education-data-shows-about-students-with-disabilities-in-the-us/

PMC. (2021). Behavior interventions in inclusive classrooms. Retrieved from https://www.ncbi.nlm.nih.gov/pmc/articles/PMC8116690/

U.S. Department of Education. (n.d.). Individuals with Disabilities Education Act (IDEA). Retrieved from https://sites.ed.gov/idea/regs/b/a/300.8/c/9

U.S. Department of Education. (n.d.). Legal rights of students with disabilities. Retrieved from https://sites.ed.gov/idea/

www.ingramcontent.com/pod-product-compliance
Lightning Source LLC
Chambersburg PA
CBHW061800120626
46550CB00005B/2074